RELIGION AND SOCIETY: NEW PERSPECTIVES FROM TURKEY

Publications of Presidency of Religious Affairs / 647
Academic Books / 107

Cover Design
Hasan KARACA

Graphic
Recep KAYA
Hüseyin DİL

Printing
Erce Matbaacılık
Tel: (0312) 394 05 65

2006-06-Y-0003-647
ISBN: 975-19-3864-3

PUBLICATIONS of PRESIDENCY of RELIGIOUS AFFAIRS

To Professor William Graham with many thanks...

23 April 2008

RELIGION AND SOCIETY: NEW PERSPECTIVES FROM TURKEY

Professor Ali Bardakoğlu
President of Religious Affairs

ANKARA - 2006

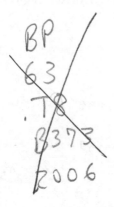

This book was printed in accordance with the decision (date 30/03/2006, no: 72) of Supreme Assembly of Religious Affairs.

CONTENTS

Foreword

This book is a collection of papers presented at international conferences, keynote speeches at invited meetings and a lengthy newspaper interview. Articles and speeches in this book address a number of important and timely questions on the administration of religious affairs, authority of religious knowledge, Islam and democracy, state-religion relations, peace and conflict resolution. The book begins with an article on "The Structure, Mission and Social Function of the Presidency of Religious Affairs" in Turkey to explain the context for following discussions.

Current developments and recent social and cultural transformations under the forces of globalization indicate that previously established casual connection between the beginning of modernity and the decline of traditional forms of religious life did not prove right in many parts of the globe. Transnational networks and the communication revolution enabled religion to become a global reality in the world. There is an increasing interest in the social role of religion because of continuing influence of the sacred in contemporary society. We live in an interdependent world and need to pay closer attention to the challenges and opportunities of social changes at the global level which may influence relations between religion, state and society. In order to understand the position of religion today, we should examine the larger dynamics of economic, cultural and political transformations. Scholars and thinkers spend tremendous effort to analyze the nature and transformation of religion both in its traditional and modern forms. This book is an attempt to locate religion in its current context and provide an analysis as far as Islam is concerned with special emphasis on Turkey.

The Presidency of Religious Affairs has an enormous responsibility in the administration of religious services in modern Turkey. This book includes papers and speeches addressing various aspects of the Presidency of Religious Affairs to demonstrate the fact that it cannot remain indifferent to vital issues concerning various aspects of religion which is a strong social reality today. I share my views and visions in this book in the capacity of a scholar working on Islam for more than twenty years and as well as the President of Religious Affairs. I hope that readers will have a better understanding of the position of the Presidency of Religious Affairs, religion and society, Islam and democracy and co-existence differences in Turkey. The book ends with appendixes which include samples of press releases by the Presidency of Religious Affairs to indicate that the Presidency did not remain silent on issues and questions which are related to religious symbols and discourses.

I would like to thank to the organizers and participants of the conferences and meetings which provided me with an excellent opportunity to discuss my views with a distinguished audience. I also thank Talip Küçükcan, Ali Köse, Hadi Adanalı, Hayrettin Yücesoy and Şemsettin Ulusal for their contribution in the preparation of this book.

Professor Ali Bardakoğlu
President of Religious Affairs

The Structure, Mission and Social Function of the Presidency of Religious Affairs*

It is useful to present an overview of the historical origins of the Presidency of Religious Affairs before moving on to its structure, legal basis, social and institutional functions. The Presidency of Religious Affairs is not a novelty in Turkey; its roots can be found in Ottoman history. The Presidency, which is a modern expression of our culture and civilization, can be associated with our past.

a) It would be wrong to claim that the Presidency of Religious Affairs is a continuation of the Ottoman institution of *Şeyhülis-lâmlık* (the office of the *Şeyhülislam*) or its structure.[1] These two institutions differ in terms of their functions and mandates. Nevertheless, in Ottoman society, the relations between religion and politics and the organization of religious affairs were regulated under the authority of the institution of *Şeyhülislâmlık* which was granted a certain degree of autonomy. This was largely preserved and continued during the Republican period with some limitations in the field of authority. In fact, in the Ottoman system, the head of the religious administration was not the Şeyhülislam, but rather the Sultan. The Şeyhülislam administered religious affairs on behalf of the Sultan.

---

* This paper was presented at the Conference on "Religion, State and Society in Turkey and Europe" organized by Konrad-Adenauer-Stiftung and the Goethe Institute in Istanbul on 23-24 October 2003, and later published in the Turkish Policy Quarterly, Spring 2004, pp. 29-37

1 For more information on the institution of Şeyhülislam *see* Esra Yakut, *Şeyhülislamlık: Yenileşme Döneminde Devlet ve Din*, İstanbul: Kitap Yayınevi, 2005; Murat Akgündüz , *XIX. Asır Başlarına Kadar Osmanlı Devletinde Şeyhülislamlık*, Unpublished PhD Thesis, Marmara Üniversitesi Sosyal Bilimler Enstitüsü İslam Tarihi ve Sanatları Anabilim Dalı, 1999.

The *kaza* (office of the Kadi[2] - judges) system and the kadis in the Ottoman Empire also deserve some attention in this context. Professor İlber Ortaylı[3] has carried out a major series of research projects in this subject. The Ottoman kadis reported to the Sheikh-ul-Islam, but served in a multi-functional post that included both judicial and municipal services in the present sense. Religious education was a major area of activity for the office of the Sheikh-ul-Islam and the kadis, while all of these functions were separated in the Republican period, with religious education and training being annexed to the Ministry of Education. In the past there was a Ministry of *Şer'iye ve Evkaf* (Religious Affairs and Charitable Foundations), but later on charitable foundations were separated from the ministry as an independent division. The Presidency of Religious Affairs was also created with a new structure under the Republican system as the institution that carried out religious affairs in society, which informed society about religion and administered places of worship.

The Presidency of Religious Affairs, which was created in the Republican period, continued the Ottoman experience to a certain extent, but was given a structure that complied with the secular structure of the state; it was given the mandate to carry out religious affairs pertaining to faith, worship and moral principles, to inform society on religion and to administer places of worship.

b) I would like to dwell upon the term *diyanet* (piety) that is used in the Turkish title of the Presidency in a few sentences. In classical religious literature *diyanet* is used as an antonym of *kaza*, i.e. the judiciary. *Kaza* expresses the judiciary and the process by which legal, political and administrative relations among all people are regulated by worldly institutions through worldly sanctions, while

---

2 For more information on the institution of Kadılık, *see* Yaşar Şahin Anıl, *Osmanlıda Kadılık*, Istanbul: İletişim Yayınları, 1993.

3 İlber Ortaylı, *Osmanlı Devletinde Kadı: hukuk ve idare adamı olarak*, Ankara: Turhan Kitabevi, 1994.

diyanet expresses a higher value; the spiritual and moral aspects of life. In other words, *kaza* is a judgment made by the judiciary in the present sense and *diyanet* is the process by which people discuss and evaluate their own actions within their hearts and also take heed of their responsibilities before God. Sometimes the decisions of the judiciary do not satisfy people. They can go beyond the strict and normative approaches of the judiciary in their internal world. So the term *diyanet* signifies the consistency, integrity and spiritual piety in a person's internal world. In that sense, the choice of the word *diyanet* in the Republican period, rather than simply using the term 'religious affairs' – *din işleri* – can be interpreted as an effort to provide for religiousness based on a moral foundation. Other interpretations can also be made, but this is the one that I favor most.

c) There is another point that should be mentioned: there is a thesis that suggests that there is no clergy in Islam. However, this thesis should not be exaggerated or severed from historical facts. The absence of clergy in Islam means that there is no special class equipped with holy abilities to speak on behalf of God and religion. Yet, since the early days of the Prophet, there have been imams and religious officials who render religious services and administer practices of worship in society. The idea which suggests that there is no clergy in Islam is a higher, more theological idea that pertains to the origins of theology and the message conveyed by religion in the world. On the other hand, the presence of a class that renders religious services relates to practical life, and in this sense there has always been a class of religious officials. The organization of this class has been shaped by the social structures, institutional culture and the traditions of society; it has existed in various forms, such as independent, free, semi-public or public.

In this sense, the concept of *diyanet* does not contradict the idea of there being no clergy in Islam. Rather, it covers the social organization of religious officials and services and the maintenance of public stability and strength in the field of religion. Therefore, the absence of clergy in Islamic theology does not mean that religious services were delivered in a haphazard fashion or that they were not subject to any controls or organization in the historical experience of Muslim societies.

d) There are three major features of the Presidency of Religious Affairs: its public, free and civilian nature.

1. In terms of its structure, the Presidency of Religious Affairs is a public institution. In other words, it is located within the state organization. Lawyers and scholars have always debated whether this contradicts the secular structure of the state. In fact, this has to do with the way one views secularism. I would like to refer to the special assessment of the Constitutional Court concerning why secularism and the Presidency of Religious Affairs do not contradict each other.

As a result of its deliberations, the Constitutional Court concluded that the public structure of the Presidency of Religious Affairs does not contradict the principle of secularism. How do we perceive secularism then? Secularism is respect shown for religious affairs by the state and the lack of religious intervention in state affairs. However, this does not mean a total severance of the two. Secularism does not entail total independence and operation in two separate areas. As the Ottoman example illustrates, it is rather a relationship based on mutual respect and balance. In other words, it is an approach that prevents domination, but enables communication, solidarity and cooperation towards developing society further. In conclusion, the Constitutional Court declared that the structure of the Presidency of Religious Affairs does not contradict secularism, basing its judgment on the following facts:

aa. Religion does not dominate or influence state affairs.

bb. Unlimited and non-discriminatory freedom is granted to the spiritual lives of all individuals, thus providing a constitutional guarantee to religious rights.

cc. In order to protect public order and interest, provisions are made to limit religious actions and behavior that go beyond the spiritual world of the individual and which have an effect on social life.

dd. The state is given supervisory powers over religious rights and liberties as the guardian of public order and public rights.

Judgment is based on the guarantee extended by the state for religious freedom and the supervision carried out on religious demands in order to prevent them from violating social order. It is also based on an attempt to balance religiously-inspired public demands of individuals in the field of public liberties. Providing sound information on religion to society, regulating the organization of religious affairs or meeting the demands of the citizens in this field are among the major aims of the Presidency of Religious Affairs. The public nature of the Presidency of Religious Affairs stems from organizational aspects. What matters is the kind of religious services the Presidency of Religious Affairs shall render and the kind of information it will produce during the rendering of these services. The question on the discourse the Presidency shall use while propounding religion or while informing the public has nothing to do with its public nature. It becomes public nature when the organization is required by public power or when the public is provided for during the rendering of religious services and in the establishment of the balance of other demands and freedoms.

2. The second aspect of the Presidency of Religious Affairs is that it is free to choose the scholarly and religious discourse it will use. Indeed, no matter how different things may appear, I can safely say that during my term of office and in my area of activity, the Presidency of Religious Affairs has acted totally on its own initiative, its own scholarly competence and accumulation of knowledge and with Turkey's scholarly capacity while providing religious services, responding to religious questions that come from the citizens or informing people of religious issues. It has also paid atten-

tion to selecting the most accurate, the soundest and the most enlightening summaries and interpretations and to remaining independent and original. This is what is required by the interpretation of the principle of secularism, as the way a secular state interprets religion is not to display a preference in the religious discourse to be used, but rather to provide freedom to individuals and their collective organizations in the public sphere. A state definition of religion would mean a significant contradiction of secularism. The information on which the Presidency of Religious Affairs relies while rendering religious services, the religious interpretations it develops, chooses and produces while enlightening the people, are directly connected to the capacity in Turkey, the personal and institutional competence of individuals and the accumulation of knowledge in Turkey, and even in the Islamic world.

Of course we cannot claim that all expectations and hopes have been fulfilled. This depends on the nature of religious knowledge and the enormous possibility for interpretation in Islam. Looking back at fourteen centuries of Islamic tradition, it becomes clear that religion has clear provisions, but there have emerged regional and geographical differences in religious traditions, allowing religious practices to vary.

Moreover, intellect, individual initiative and interpretation all play a special and exclusive role in Islam. However, this broad possibility for interpretation does not mean that Islam is ambiguous, that it is completely open to interpretation or that it can evolve in different ways through personal interpretations. No matter how open Islam may be to interpretation, it is the holy texts that define the limits of interpretation. Therefore, the holy texts and the authentic structure of Islam include both the possibility and the impossibility for interpretation. We regard religion as a sociological phenomenon, as an experience that reflects daily life, something that people live and experience and that serves the common interests of people rather than a science fiction narrative constructed and produced at a desk. This is the reason why the Presidency of Religious Affairs always acts on free information in its mission to enlighten the public, why it produces knowledge freely and abstains from extreme or paradoxical explanations. Our religious tradition and our historical religious experience thus remind us that we operate within an area of limited freedom.

Let me reiterate here that these limitations stem from the nature of the religion, the possibility granted by the religious texts and our historical experience. These limitations are not set by its public nature. However, people have false expectations or misconceptions, and they may link the reserved and cautious approach of the Presidency in rendering religious services, or of the theology faculties or the religious scholars in offering interpretations with this public nature. Both the Presidency of Religious Affairs and the theology faculties act in a consistent fashion, in that they are somewhat reserved in their religious interpretations and rarely go outside of mainstream interpretations. This originates not from the public nature or the public concept of religion in Turkey, but from Islamic methodology and a consistency of generating religious information.

3. The third feature of the Presidency of Religious Affairs is its civilian nature that derives from democracy. Since the majority in Turkey is Muslim, they need to be able to fulfill their religious needs and to practice their religion freely, equipped with true and accurate information; such institutions as the Presidency have emerged independently. In other words, the Presidency of Religious Affairs is an institution that is both democratic and civilian. It is not a hierarchical institution that is detached from the real religious life or the demands of the people. So, while we render the services of the Presidency of Religious Affairs, deliver religious services and inform the society about religion, we also take our scholarly freedom into account and pay attention to remaining loyal to the Islamic methodology established by the learned generations. We also take into consideration the experience of the Islam of our people, as well

as their demands and inclinations. This is a process of education. That is why the Presidency of Religious Affairs does not follow extreme ideas nor implement them, but rather pursues stable experiences that have been tried and proven to bring peace, trust and order to society. The most striking difference between an academic institution and the Presidency of Religious Affairs perhaps lies here.

We regard the Presidency of Religious Affairs as an institution which takes the religious demands and traditions of people into account, and if there are any diversions from these, one which tries to improve them with true and authentic religious knowledge; this is an institution that tries to inform our people by providing them with training and education under the light of a scientific and sound religious knowledge. To us, the Presidency of Religious Affairs is not an institution that disturbs or offends people, nor does it condemn their religious experiences or preferences, nor denounce them. Neither is it an institution that attempts to impose a certain model of religiousness on people. This is the civilian aspect of the Presidency of Religious Affairs. At this point, both the sensitivities of the public sphere and the sensitivities of a free and civil society should be taken into account. The three aspects I referred to above define the structure and function of the Presidency of Religious Affairs today. They further enable us to see the minefield in which it operates.

e) In the tradition of Islam, scholars have taken pains to give a certain shape to social order, public stability and public opinion. Knowledge lies at the foundation of society. Therefore, a Muslim society is one that generates sound knowledge, rejects misinformation and thus develops and takes knowledge as authority.

Indeed there is no clergy in Islam. Muslims do not derive their power, authority or dignity from sacred men and institutions. Then where do these come from? From scientific knowledge that overlaps with the main sources of religion which are derived from tradition and interpreted according to the needs of the time. However, this is not a positive science. It is a form of knowledge that is authentic, free and sound within its own methodology. Therefore, the Presidency of Religious Affairs needs to strike a fine balance between its knowledge-based freedom and respect for civil initiative. For the Presidency it is equally important to protect scholarly freedom and civil initiative as it is to take into account public sensitivity and neutrality that have been brought about by its public nature.

Sound knowledge means a struggle against superstition, error, ignorance, injustice and religious abuse. In the Islamic tradition, it has been theologians that have been the ones who have continued the struggle against injustice, superstition, abuse and fanaticism. Religious knowledge involves this kind of a struggle in its very heart. By basing its actions on sound religious knowledge and information, the Presidency of Religious Affairs does not tolerate hard-line tendencies that disturb social peace, and proceeds to educate, convince and inform people who have such tendencies. This is a minefield full of risks. Piety, which is based on emotion rather than knowledge, usually remains reserved and withdrawn. It becomes nearly impossible to enlighten people who have surrendered to a certain force, movement or center of attraction in an emotional atmosphere with sound knowledge. In Turkey, the Presidency of Religious Affairs and the theology faculties are responsible for this near-impossible task. Under these circumstances, success is achieved with great difficulty and failure is almost invariably seen to be the fault of the Presidency of Religious Affairs and the theology faculties. Indeed, it is very difficult to achieve success in this field. It is difficult to tell the educators that they too need to be educated and it is equally difficult to test and challenge the knowledge of people who see and define themselves as true devout Muslims. Despite everything, centers of religious knowledge and the Presidency of Religious Affairs have managed to attain a level of success in this difficult task. Complete success is not possible, in any case. We need to see things from a more optimistic perspective. I have always seen life and its events in a positive light. In conclusion, I can safely state that a sound religious tradition and understanding have been established in Turkey after numerous experiences.

f) The piety and religious experiences of Turkey play a very important role and constitute an exemplary experience. Both due to its dynamism and transparency and due to its political flexibility and secularity, Turkey's piety and view of religion constitute a special example and an experience which provides a major opportunity for the West to examine. I sincerely think and believe that the Turkish experience has a great deal to contribute if we want to liberate religion from being the source and cause of violence, tension and disagreement and if we desire to establish a common ground for peace.

When I refer to dialogue, I mean realizing our differences and coexisting without exaggerating and worrying about them. To me, creating uniform and heterogeneous groups of people with no significant differences is not the way to establish dialogue. What is essential is that we love each other despite our differences. There are very good examples of this in our history and traditional culture. Apart from the negative and much-debated examples of people and groups that are perceived as being the image of Islam in the West, there are also many positive examples. We have examples of people such as Mevlana (Rumi),[4] Yunus Emre[5] and Hacı Bektaş Veli[6] who extended a loving and peaceful message to the whole world.

---

4 On Rumi *see* Annemarie Schimmel, *The Triumphal Sun: A Study of the Works of Jalaloddin Rumi*, London: East and West Publishing, 1980; Seyyed Hossein Nasr, *Rumi and the Sufi Tradition*, Tehran: RCD Cultural Institute, 1974; F. D. Lewis, *Rumi: Past and Present East and West*, Oxford: Oneworld, 2000.

5 *See* Talat S. Hamlan and İlhan Başgöz (eds.), *Yunus Emre and His Mystical Poetry*, Bloomington: Indiana University, 1981; Abdülbaki Gölpınarlı, *Yunus Emre ve Tasavvuf*, Istanbul: Remzi Kitabevi, 1961.

6 See Abdülkadir Sezgin, Hacı Bektaş Veli ve Bektaşilik , Ankara: Kültür Bakanlığı, 1990; Hülya Küçük, *The Role of the Bektashis in Turkey's National Struggle: A Historical and Critical Study*, Leiden: E.J. Brill, 2002; John Kingsley Birge, *The Bektashi Order of Dervishes*, London: Luzac Oriental, 1994.

We have the responsibility to show and promote these examples and the West is responsible for taking the time to become better acquainted with them. Nevertheless, religions can always be manipulated and seen as a source of violence if they are not properly understood or propounded well. This is not only true for Islam, but also for Christianity and Judaism. The respective histories of Christianity and Judaism are full of bitter examples of this fact.[7]

g) We can overcome these problems by developing differences in positive ways and by establishing a communication network that will prevent religions from becoming sources of unease, tension, unrest and violence. We cannot claim that violence, tension and unease have no relationship to religion. Yet we should take heed of two potential mistakes. Firstly, a lack of religious education and training will have grave and serious negative consequences. This will make it impossible for societies to enjoy the positive contribution of religion to social development. Secondly, religion should not be used to attain national or international interests, for instance in order to reach expansionist targets. These mistakes often follow from one another.

h) Our need to listen to and understand each other is undeniable. This is an aspect that is always necessary, because where there is knowledge there will always be self-confidence and freedom. A knowledgeable person is one who has self-confidence and who is able to leave a sphere of freedom for others. The road to freedom progresses through self-confidence. Persons or systems without self-confidence will also restrict the spheres of freedom. The production and updating of knowledge through sound, accurate and dynamic methods is indispensable if we are to develop our

---

7 *See* Henry O. Thompson, *World Religions in War and Peace*, Horth Carolina: Mcfarland And Co., 1988; John Ferguson, *War and Peace in the World's Religions*, New York: Oxford University, 1978; David R. Smock, *Religious Perspectives on War: Christian, Muslim and Jewish Attitudes Toward Force After the Gulf War*, Washington: United States Institute of Peace, 1992.

European Union policies and international dialogue. In other words, religious knowledge should take on a form that will bring peace, trust and the joy of peaceful co-existence. We all have many things that we must do and learn from each other in this respect.

j) At the Presidency of Religious Affairs, we aim to produce a service policy that embraces all of our population. Our human nature is our common denominator and our common identity. In terms of the services rendered by the Presidency of Religious Affairs, Islam is our common identity. We have adopted the goal of embracing all people, regardless of their religious awareness, striving to serve and inform them. This is required by our interests, knowledge and our experience. This goal also covers members of other religions.

Emphasizing the free and civilian nature of the Presidency, rather than its public structure, I would like to state that my greatest wish is to see everyone practicing their own religion, following their own school of thought or cultural tendencies freely in this land. I have gained the impression from my contacts with other religious leaders that they desire the same thing. They have also displayed the same positive attitude. Then let us reciprocally take the required steps toward religious freedom.[8] But we want the same freedom with the same sensitivities to be granted to Muslims and others in Europe, in the Balkans, in Western Thrace and everywhere else in the world. No matter where one may be in the world or which religion one belongs to, we should all assist those who cannot practice their religions freely. I am happy to see that everyone has reached a certain level of awareness about this issue. I hope that this awareness will be our common point of departure and that we will make use of every opportunity to fulfill the responsibility we have to ourselves, our societies and the whole of humanity.

---

8 For an excellent study on this issue see Tore Lindholm, W. Cole Durham and Bahia G. Tahzib-Lie (eds), *Facilitating Freedom of Religion or Belief: A Deskbook*, Leiden: Nijhoff, 2005.

Moderate Perception of Islam
and the Turkish Model of Diyanet*

Introduction

Modern Turkey is trying to find a balance between religion and secularism by constantly improving its democratic culture. In my opinion, Turkey offers an excellent case study to find the answers to the following questions: What makes Turkey different from other Muslim countries? What are the sources of moderate perception and understanding of Islam in Turkey? Can Islam and democracy coexist? How far can democracy establish freedom for religious diversity? I will try to answer these questions in my paper.

There are a number of agents and institutions in Turkey which contribute to the debate on how Islam is perceived, understood and practiced in society. Broadly speaking, we can divide these individuals and institutions into three categories: (a) official agents and institutions, such as public and private educational institutions; (b) nonofficial agents and institutions, such as religious and civil organizations and networks; (c) the mass media (TV channels and newspapers), books, magazines and communication networks, such as the internet. All of these agents, to various degrees, play a role in

---

*   This paper was presented at the international conference on "Moderation in Islam" organized by Middle East Center, University of Utah, USA on 21-22 February 2004; it was later published under the title "Moderate Perception of Islam and the Turkish Model of Diyanet: The President's Statement" in the Journal of Muslim Minority Affairs, vol. 24, No. 2, October 2004.

the promotion and transmission of religious knowledge to the public. There is no doubt that the content and methods of such transmissions have an impact on how Islam is perceived by the masses. It would be a very useful exercise to examine the role of these agents and their impact on how Islam is perceived in modern Turkey. However, in this paper I will only offer some thoughts concerning the role of the Presidency of Religious Affairs, known in Turkey as the Diyanet.

The Organization of Religious Service

The Diyanet has a particular role as a public institution in the production and transmission of religious knowledge. It holds the responsibility of organizing and providing religious services to Muslims in Turkey. Indeed, without understanding the role and function of the Diyanet, our analysis of religion and society in Turkey will remain incomplete. Therefore, I will briefly touch upon public, civil and independent characteristics of the Diyanet as a large and effective institution. I will review the transition from the Ottoman Empire to the modern Turkish Republic, as far as the management of religious affairs and its links to the state and politics are concerned.

Although the Sultan, as head of state, in theory had political and religious authority, in the Ottoman Empire religious affairs were run by a Şeyhülislam on behalf of the Sultan and the state. The state provided the means and independence for the Şeyhülislam to organize and administrate religious affairs. In short, the state took responsibility for the organization and administration of religious affairs via the office of the Şeyhülislam.

However, responsibility and authority of the state as distributed during the Ottoman Empire were passed to the modern Republic of Turkey in a different way. Here, one can see a certain degree of historical continuity in state-religion relations in terms of existence of an institutional body responsible for delivering religious services, although it differs in its legal and administrative structures.

In modern Turkey, the state also claims the responsibility for the organization and administration of religious affairs. However, during the transition from the Ottoman Empire to a secular republic, the Diyanet was established as a public institution.[1] It was intended that the Ottoman methods should be continued to some extent, and that such activities would be in conformity with the secular structure of the state. The Diyanet was made responsible for the administration of religious affairs in the areas of Islamic faith, practices and moral principles. The organization of mosques and informing people about Islam also became primary responsibilities of the Diyanet. When we look at the aims and the organization of the Diyanet, we can see that it did not merely emerge as a bureaucratic institution, but rather as part of a project to establish moral religiosity.

Here I should also point out that there is frequent mention of the argument that there is no clergy in Islam. Yet, from the formative period of Islam on there has been a special group of people and scholars who have conducted religious affairs, such as leading prayers and teaching Islam. Religious services emerged as an aspect of practical daily life and a number of people were charged or claimed responsibility for the provision of such services. The emergence and organization of people who were to be responsible for the provision of religious services took place according to the social structures and political realities of Muslim societies. Furthermore, dominant cultures and customs also helped to shape the institutions which became responsible for the day to day run-

---

1 There are a number of works on Diyanet in Turkish. *See* for example, İştar B. Tarhanlı, *Müslüman Toplum "laik" Devlet: Türkiye'de Diyanet İşleri Başkanlığı* Istanbul: Afa Yayınları, 1993; Kamil Kaya, *Sosyolojik Açıdan Türkiye'de Din-Devlet İlişkileri ve Diyanet İşleri Başkanlığı,* Istanbul: Emre Matbaası, 1998, Ruşen Çakır, İrfan Bozan, *Sivil, Şeffaf ve Demokratik Bir Diyanet İşleri Başkanlığı Mümkün mü?* Istanbul: Türkiye Ekonomik ve Sosyal Etüdler Vakfı, 2005.

ning of religious affairs and the provision of religious services in the Muslim world.

Dependent on these factors, civil, independent, semi-public and public institutions emerged to organize and administer religious affairs. In Turkey, the establishment of the Diyanet with its current status and function is not in contradiction with the idea that there is no clergy in Islam. We can argue that the Diyanet emerged as a response to a social need for the organization of religious affairs and in order to provide religious services.

The establishment of the Diyanet can also be seen as a response to the problem of sustaining public stability in the area of religious affairs and as a way to meet the public demand for satisfactory religious services. Here, I would like to underline the fact that the absence of a clergy in Islam does not mean that religious affairs are administered casually or that religious services are provided in a disorganized manner in Muslim societies.

Characteristics of the Diyanet

The organizational structure and functions of the Diyanet can be categorized as follows:

The Diyanet as a Public Institution

By structure, the Diyanet is a public institution; it is part of the state machinery and the bureaucratic system. The Diyanet's place in the state organization and whether this contradicts the secular nature of the state has been an ongoing controversial issue among legal experts and scholars in Turkey. This issue is related to how one understands secularism. The position of the Diyanet within the state organization is not in contradiction with secularism, according to the following principles that are upheld in Turkey: (a) Religions should not be dominant or effective agents in state affairs. (b) The provision of unrestricted freedom for the religious beliefs of individuals and religious liberty are under constitutional protection. (c) The prevention of the misuse and exploitation of religion is essential for the protection of the public interest. (d) The state has authority to ensure the provision of religious rights and freedoms as the protector of public order and rights.

What we see here is the protection of religious liberties on the one hand, while at the same time there is a mechanism to control the expression of religious demands that might threaten social order. There is also a principle here that is concerned with public rights, aimed at establishing a balanced policy regarding public demands that stem from religious matters.

Providing sound religious information and the organization of religious affairs and making efforts to meet the needs of citizens are important duties for modern societies. The public character of the Diyanet relates to its organizational affairs. The Diyanet's public dimension is not related to how it will produce religious knowledge or illuminate people in religious matters. Its public character pertains to the fact that it provides an organizational structure and policy, which is required by public order, while rendering religious services. Its public character also pertains to establishing a balance between demands and freedoms.

The Diyanet as an Independent Institution

The Diyanet is an independent (public) institution and enjoys freedom in scholarly activities, in intellectual discussions of Islamic issues, in the production of religious knowledge and its dissemination to the public. I would like to emphasize that, no matter how it may appear from outside, the Diyanet under my presidency conducts its affairs freely without any restriction when providing religious services.

The Diyanet plans and executes its policies and practices based on scholarly findings and experience. Utmost care is given in making the best choices and finding the most original solutions among all available interpretations, without external pressures. At this point I would like to draw the reader's attention to our understanding of secularism. Here, secularism does not mean the intervention of the state in the interpretation of religion. Nor does it imply state intervention into how a religion should be explained or communicated to the people.

Secularism does not call for an interpretation of religion by the state. Rather, it provides freedom to individuals and to public institutions in the interpretation of religion and in the production and transmission of religious knowledge. The definition of religion by the state will contradict the very essence of secularism. Therefore, the Diyanet exercises scholarly and intellectual freedom in regard to these matters, as its religious interpretations used when informing people and providing religious services, are all related to individual and institutional capacity and to the experiences of those involved in Turkey and even extends to those in the Muslim world.

One of the original aspects of the Diyanet's approach to religion and its interpretation is the fact that it sees religion as more than a mere theoretical belief system. As we know, the interpretation of Islam varies according to geographical areas and the dominant local traditions and cultures. Therefore, religion is seen to some extent a social experience and a sociological phenomenon. Sociological facts, historical legacy and experiences explain the boundaries of freedom in the organization of religious affairs; this is the challenge facing the Diyanet today.

These sociological realities and traditions draw the boundaries of how far an institution can be free in interpreting religion. Such factors indicate that our freedom is limited. However, this restriction does not stem from religious texts, but rather from traditions and historical legacies. Thus, this restriction is not embedded in the public character of the institution itself. There is a wide but misconceived tendency in Turkey on the part of some people to explain the religious services of the Diyanet and the hesitant behaviour of scholars at theological faculties to interpret the religion in relation to the "public" structure, i.e. the state. In my view, the sensitivity of the Diyanet and the hesitancy of scholars in interpreting the religion and the conformity of their views to the main body of scholarship should not be attributed to their links with the "public" structure or to the public nature of these institutions. Such positions are related to the methodology of producing Islamic knowledge.

The Diyanet as a Civil Institution

The third characteristic of the Diyanet is its civil nature which is a result of democracy. The Diyanet emerged as a response to the religious needs of Muslim believers. Turkey has a predominantly Muslim population and the people need to learn about their religion freely in the light of authentic scholarship. The Diyanet was established to meet such needs in society; it therefore has a democratic and civil basis.

The Diyanet did not emerge without having any relation to the demands and needs that pertain to the religious life of Turkish society. Thus, while providing religious services and informing people about their religion, the Diyanet takes their demands, their traditions and their experiences into account while it preserves its scholarly independence. The Diyanet pursues stable ideas and experiences which ensure social peace and trust. It promotes such aspects of religious experience; it does not promote extreme ideas. This makes the Diyanet rather different from an academic institution.

The Diyanet does not pursue a policy of causing injury to people's beliefs, or undermining their experiences of religiosity or their preferences. The Diyanet does not despise what the public believe and practice today. In that sense, the Diyanet does not have a policy of imposing a particular model of religiosity on people. The Diyanet does not support an essentialist idea of Islam.

The Diyanet takes religious demands and traditional forms into account when delivering its services. However, if and when there is a departure from the shared and sustained perception, the Diyanet then promotes authentic knowledge; it strives to educate people about their religious beliefs and practices in the light of sound knowledge and scholarship. It is in this that the civil nature of the Diyanet lies. At this juncture, an observation of civil demands and freedom is as important as an observation of public concerns (concerns of the state).

These three (public, independent and civil) aspects of the Diyanet explain its current structure and function. They also indicate that the Diyanet faces numerous challenges as an institution. As I noted earlier, there is no clergy, a special class for religious matters in Islam. However, that doesn't mean absence of a scholarly authority. As there is no system of clergy in Islam, then where do Muslims scholars derive their authority, power and respect from? They derive these from the knowledge and interpretation of the tradition which conforms to authentic sources of Islam. The Diyanet derives its independence from its expertise in Islamic knowledge and scholarship. However, it has to establish a balance between its independence and its respect for civil initiatives. For the Diyanet, it is important to observe its public structure as a state organization, as well as its scientific (scholarly) independence and its pursuits of civil concerns in Turkish society.

Sound knowledge helps in fighting superstitions, ignorance, false ideas, misuses of religion and abuses in the name of religion. In Islamic history, Muslim scholars took responsibility for fighting superstitions, ignorance and fanaticism. They took this responsibility because religious knowledge requires, by its very nature, such a struggle. The Diyanet gives priority to providing healthy and sound religious knowledge to society. The intention in doing this is to educate people and to promote the tolerance of various religious trends in society. The Diyanet promotes a religiosity based on scholarship, sound knowledge and interpretation. Sentimental religiosity is introverted, and closed to the external world. Sentimental religiosity may lead to total self closure, and for such people it will be difficult to open their minds to critical thinking.

Turkey's Unique Position among Muslim Countries

Modern Turkey has a unique place among modern Muslim nation states. Turkey lies at the crossroads between Eastern and Western civilizations. Turkey has the privilege of having a history which contains the diverse cultural and religious traditions of both the East and the West. These multiple traditions have played a major role in the construction of the political and cultural identity of Turkish society. Both domestic and external forces that have existed in and around Turkey over the centuries have had their effects.[2]

Modern Turkey was established on the ruins of the Ottoman Empire and inherited an imperial legacy. The Ottomans launched modern reforms during the eighteenth century in political, legal, administrative, educational, and cultural fields. The founders of the republic of Turkey adopted these reforms and pursued the modernization process in Turkish society. Although some of the reforms in the early republican period caused a cultural rupture, the resources and cultural references that make up Turkey's unique identity were preserved in the fabric of society.[3]

As Bernard Lewis points out, despite the striking changes that Turkish society has faced, the Islamic imprint still remains alive:

"Islam has profound roots among the Turkish people. From its

---

2 T. Kucukcan, "State, Islam and Religious Liberty in Modern Turkey: Reconfiguration of Religion in the Public Sphere", *Brigham Young University Law Review*, Volume 2003, No: 2, 2003, p. 475.

3 For a detailed examination of the imperial legacy on Turkish Republic *see* M. Meeker, *A Nation of Empire the Ottoman Legacy of Turkish Modernity*, Berkeley: California University Press, 2002, pp. 3-85 and pp. 372-396.

foundation until its fall the Ottoman Empire was a state dedicated to the advancement or defence of the power and faith of Islam...After a century of Westernization, Turkey has undergone immense changes greater than any outside observer had thought possible. But the deepest Islamic roots of Turkish life and culture are still alive, and the ultimate identity of Turk and Muslim in Turkey is still unchallenged."[4]

Although the majority of the population in Turkey is Muslim, Islam is not a monolithic religion in this society. The majority of the Muslim population belongs to the loosely defined Sunni interpretation of Islam. But the current perception and practice of Islam varies from mystical and folk Islam to conservative and more moderate understanding of Islam. This situation is a result of the exposure of Turkish society to various cultural currents throughout the centuries. The Diyanet acknowledges this diversity and promotes a moderate, tolerant and embracing perception of Islam. Several non-Muslim religious groups also exist in Turkey. Most of them are concentrated in Istanbul and in other large cities.[5] Their existence adds to the great diversity which we enjoy today in Turkey.

Turkey Projects a Moderate Perception of Islam

Today, Turkey emerges a country that supports a moderate, tolerant and inclusive perception of Islam. The widespread perception of Islam in Turkey is not radical, fundamentalist or exclusive. One of the reasons for such a moderate understanding of Islam in Turkish society is the fact that democracy has existed in Turkey for more than eighty years. Since its establishment, Turkey has improved its democracy and now it represents a successful experience in the world. What we see in Turkey is that democratic culture promotes tolerance, participation, civil society and moderation. It is clear that other Muslim countries and societies also need democra-

---

4 B. Lewis, *The Emergence of Modern Turkey*, London: Oxford University Press, 1961, p. 418.
5 For estimated numbers of non-Muslims in Turkey *see* T. Kucukcan, *op. cit.*, p. 502.

cy, transparency and participation more than at any other period in history.

When we look at the Muslim world today, we see numerous problems regarding democratization and state-religion relations. We see that in some countries Islam is used to justify non-democratic politics and authoritarian regimes. It is time to take a critical look at the problem of the misuse of Islam for political justification. Islam promotes human rights, political participation, civil initiatives, and justice and equality; it does not oppress ideas in the name of God. If we have a moderate perception of Islam in Turkey, we owe this to the establishment of the democratic culture in Turkey, despite all the problems.

I would like to point out that moderate perception of Islam in Turkey is also rooted in the fact that different trends, ideas and views of Islam can be expressed in Turkey. As I mentioned earlier, the majority of the Turkish population are Muslims. But Islam does not have a monolithic nature in Turkey.[6] The interpretation of Islam may differ from group to group. There is room for all views and interpretations.

Intellectuals, scholars and leaders of religious groups can freely express their views of Islam. There is no restriction on critical thinking in Islam, and Turkey enjoys such a diversity of views. Many other Muslim countries lack such a free platform. In some Muslim countries there is strict support only for one school of thought and there is a state policy to suppress opposition. In such places there is no liberty to express diverse interpretations of Islam. This policy produces a rigid understanding of Islam and uniformity. And such rigid, hard-line interpretations leave no room for moderation and tolerance. If this rigid and monolithic interpretation of

---

6 For an extensive analysis of the variety of religious trends and movements in Turkey *see* Hakan Yavuz, *Islamic Political Identity in Turkey*, Oxford, 2003; *Modern Türkiye'de Siyasi Düşünce: İslamcılık* (Political Thought in Modern Turkey: Islamism), Yasin Aktay (ed.), Vol. 6, Istanbul: Iletişim, 2004.

religion is enforced on people, it may in the end lead to fanaticism. This is what we see in some Muslim countries. Turkey differs greatly in this regard because there is room for all views.

Harmony between Islam and Democracy

Today, Muslims should be aware of the fact that democratic culture and democratic values do not contradict Islam.[7] The Muslim world should look at the achievements of Turkey in this field. Muslim scholars should no longer support authoritarian regimes and oppressive political cultures. They should not provide religious justification for such leaders and governments.

Moderation also requires acceptance of the co-existence of different religions. Turkey sets a good example of this, as the members of various religious communities are protected by the constitution and are seen as Turkish citizens. In the past, the Ottoman Empire showed a similar example of peaceful co-existence. Cultural diversity thrived under Ottoman rule by adopting a policy of recognition and tolerance for other cultures.[8] There is no reason why Muslims should not pursue such a policy today. Muslim scholars should promote the idea that Islam is not opposed to the presence of different religions or religious groups in a Muslim society. There should be no fear of forced conversion or Islamization for non-Muslims. Islam fully supports the idea that every one should practice his/her own religion.[9] In a similar way, the Western world should not pur-

---

7   *See* Ali Bardakoglu, "İslam ve Demokrasi Üzerine" (On Islam and Democracy), *İslamiyât*, Vol. 11, No: 2, pp. 77-84.

8   On the treatment of non-Muslim communities under the Ottomans *see* Kemal H. Karpat, "Millets and Nationality: The Roots of the Incongruity of Nation and State in the Post-Ottoman Era", in *Christians and Jews in the Ottoman Empire, The Functioning of a Plural Society Vol.1*, B. Braude and B. Lewis (eds.), New York: Holmes-Meier Publishers, 1982, p. 141-142; T. Kucukcan, *op. cit.*, pp. 480-485. For the legal status of non-Muslims in the Ottoman Empire *see* M. Macit Kenanoglu, *Osmanlı Devletinde Millet Sistemi ve Gayrimüslimlerin Hukuki Statüleri (1453-1856)*, (Millet System and The Legal Status of Non-Muslims in the Ottoman State), (Unpublished PhD Thesis, Marmara University), 2001.

9   *See* Ali Bardakoglu, "İslam Kültüründe Din ve Vicdan Özgürlüğü" (Freedeom of Religi-

sue a policy of converting Muslims or other religious communities to Christianity, nor should they lend support to such policies pursued by some organizations. Social and/or economic disadvantages and poor living conditions should not be manipulated for proselytizing.

Conclusion

In closing I would like to point out that one of the main differences between moderation and extremism is tolerance, which is embedded in moderate thinking itself. That is, moderation can tolerate the "other", but extremism does not have room for the "other". If you cannot tolerate extreme or opposing ideas and views, then your moderation may become another form of extremism in the name of moderation. Today, we not only need to moderate our current understanding of Islam or that of other religions, but we must also moderate our approach to life in total, including politics, welfare, human rights, gender equality, globalization, international relations, war and conflict.

Indeed, the perception of Islam in Turkey is one of a moderate nature. Democratic culture and democratic values have contributed to the emergence of such moderation. The moderate understanding of Islam in Turkey is reflected in the fact that other religious communities also enjoy freedom of religion. The current picture may not be perfect, but it looks far better than that of other Muslim countries.

---

on and Conscience in Islamic Culture), in *Osmanlı Devletinde Din ve Vicdan Özgürlüğü* (Freedeom of Religion and Conscience in the Ottoman Empire), Istanbul: Isav Publications, 2000, pp. 41-57.

Foundations of Living Together in Peace*

Humanity is faced by two basic problems in this world. One of these has a strong connection with factors that threaten human life in this world, like hunger, poverty, unemployment, inequality of opportunities, moral deterioration, lack of faith, oppression, inadequate health provisions, the issues of education and law, despotic methods, under-refinement of social culture, the destruction of historical and cultural values and similar negative factors faced by people. The other problem, though not less important than the previously mentioned one, is closely related to it, consisting of inadequate dialogue between individuals, a lack of tolerance, impatience with differences and issues concerning coexisting together in peace with such dissimilarities. These problems do not draw the attention of one region or nation alone, but rather are matters that concern all individuals who live on this earth.

Due to globalization, we are living in an increasingly tightening and shrinking world. With reference to studies that have been carried out, it is possible to denote globalization in two ways. Globalization, according to some studies is, "a new super-ethos situuation"[1] that is a process of building up valid merits world-wide which will affect people, cultures and societies. The other study defines globalization as an increase in the socio-cultural density, a

---

* This speech was delivered at the inauguration ceremony of the Panel organized by the UNESCO National Committee for "Living Together on the Golden Bridge" on May 24th, 2004 in Istanbul.
1 M.L Stackhouse, "General Introduction", M.L. Stackhouse, P.J. Paris (ed.), *God & Globalization, vol. 1: Religion and the Powers of the Common Life*, Harrisburg: Trinity Pres Int. 2000, p.19.

rapidly developing consciousness and the "shrinkage of the world".[2] For this reason, the social chaos which besieges humans, consisting of social injustice, hunger, poverty, malnutrition, violence, terror, corruption, ignorance and lack of faith, which all take place in this process, is not of interest to only those who are suffering from these issues alone, but to the whole of society as well. This, of course, implies the necessity of finding international permanent solutions to overcome such problems.

In addition to the socio-politic and socio-economic steps to be taken both on national and international levels, the contribution of the human religious, cultural and historical heritage in the solution of these issues is equally important. In particular, religious traditions comprise many things that are of importance among the issues that we face. Alongside the fundamentals of belief and worship, matters such as the emphasis of the principle of justice, the opposition of tyranny and discrimination and the acceptance of the sanctity of life, soul and property of individuals all have a place among the basic disciplines of all belief systems, particularly in that of universal religions.[3]

The aim of the religion that is oriented toward the individual can be summed up in two points. First, religions present everyday reality as well as the way for the salvation of the individual. All religions allege that they offer salvation for human beings, regardless of how this salvation or their perception of reality is expressed. In this way, a belief and worship system resembles a prescription written for the salvation of humanity.

The second point is that religions aim at the realization of

---

2 R. Robertson, "Globalization and the Future of Traditional Religion", M.L. Stackhouse, P.J. Paris (ed.) *God & Globalization, vol. 1: Religion and the Powers of the Common Life,* Harrisburg: Trinity Pres Int. 2000, p. 53.

3 For further discussions *see* M. Darrol Bryant, Rita H. Mataragnon (eds.), *The Many Faces of Religion and Society,* New York: Paragon House, 1985; Louis Schneider (ed.), *Religion, Culture and Society,* John Wiley & Sons, Inc., 1966.

human comfort and happiness, and they reveal the way in which this goal can be attained. In order to realize this, religions aim at making many virtues, such as justice, honesty, confidence, reliance, cooperation, affection and the avoidance of evil, dominant in a human's life; these virtues represent indispensable merits that lead to human happiness. Those who have faith in the diverse systems that contain the objectives mentioned above are obligated to join forces against any negative phenomena which might threaten the comfort or future of human beings. For this reason, we are confident that the way to protect the freedom of speech and belief of one segment of society lies in respecting the life and belief of other segments.[4]

The rich heritage which humanity has inherited in the field of culture and history and the accumulation of the vast experiences that have been offered to us are important factors which ought to be used in the process of overcoming the current crisis. In this context, it is absolutely certain that Anatolia has a unique place and function in the world in general. Anatolia has sheltered different experiences, traditions, values and concepts of humanity and has succeeded in handing these qualities down from generation to generation. It is for this reason that Anatolia represents a geography which possesses a historical heritage identical with the cultural history of humanity.

Anatolia plays the role of a bridge spanning three different fields at present in the following ways: (i) With its rich archeological and historical treasures that it has maintained successfully until today, (ii) with its ability to protect and keep different beliefs and values

---

4 On Freedom of religion and human rights *see* Natan Lerner, *Religion, Beliefs and International Human Rights*, New York: Orbis Books, 2000; E. M. Bucar and Barbara Barnett (eds.), *Does Human Rights Need God?*, Grand Rapids: William B. Eerdsmans Publishing Company, 2005; R. E. Florida, *Human Rights - The Buddhist Tradition*, Praeger, 2005; W. H. Brackney, *Human Rights - The Christian Tradition*, Praeger, 2005; H. Coward, *Human Rights –The Hindu Tradition*, 2005; M. Abd-Al-Rahim, *Human Rights - The Islamic Tradition*, Praeger, 2005; P.J. Haas, *Human Rights - The Jewish Tradition*, Praeger, 2005.

alive throughout its history (iii) and with its aptitude to establish the culture of "living together with differences" which provides a suitable environment for the traditions, understandings, ways of life and followers of diverse beliefs to coexist together in peace and tranquility.[5]

Anatolia, from one end to the other, appears as if it were an open-air museum. Moreover, it presents an endless number of archeological materials and historical values from different eras of history to humanity. The protection of such a cultural heritage, conserving it before it disappears or before it is destroyed, reflects the attitude and the self-sacrificing nature of the Anatolian people. The indigenous inhabitants of Anatolia chose to care for the historical heritage of this land rather than destroying it. They evaluated the structures and the remains of the preceding historical periods according to their own needs and they chose to carry on their functionality. In this way, the temples, structures, tools and equipment that belonged to different religions and traditions from the east to the west of Anatolia succeeded in surviving until the present time, even if they were sometimes used in different contexts.[6]

Anatolia, from the archaic period until the present time, became an area filled with cultural legacy inherited from the Hittite and Sumerian civilizations, from the Roman and Byzantium eras, from the Seljuk and Ottoman civilizations, and finally from the Republican period. The cultural heritage mentioned here has been preserved until the present time, making good use of shared experiences and utilizing what had been learned or gained, without any reciprocal destruction. In this way, Anatolia is not merely a geo-

---

5 Amin Saikal and Christine Kertesz (eds.), *Turkey: A Bridge Between East and West*, Canberra: The Australian National University, 1996.
6 Ekrem Akurgalı, *Anadolu Uygarlıkları*, Istanbul: Net Turistik Yayınları, 1993; Ferit Edgü (ed.), *Anadolu Medeniyetleri*, Istanbul, Kültür ve Turizm Bakanlığı, 1983; Derman Bayladı, *Uygarlıklar Kavşağı Anadolu*, Istanbul: Say Yayınları, 1996.

graphic bridge connecting Asia with Europe or the East with the West, but is also a perception combining the past with the present and introducing Eastern thought to the Western way of thinking.[7]

Anatolia is remarkable with its unique structure that formed the cradle for many religions, like Islam, Christianity and Judaism, allowing them to coexist together and simultaneously acting as the birthplace for many belief systems. After the 10th and 11th centuries, which witnessed intense times of migration and conversior to Islam, and even after the period which observed the conversion of the Anatolian nations to Islam, policies that were aimed at assimilating or eradicating Christianity, Judaism or similar religions were never pursued, on the contrary, the regulations put into practice by Sultan Mehmet the Conqueror after the conquest of Istanbul clearly aimed at protecting the existence of the different belief systems and communities, as well as constituting appropriate circumstances to guarantee their survival.[8] As a result, different religious groups that were living under severe oppression outside of Anatolia at that time migrated here to take shelter in this land. Here there was an atmosphere of freedom for all. The Jews, compelled to migrate to Anatolia from Spain and different European countries at the end of the 15th century, constitute the most meaningful example of such people.

Another special feature that attracts our attention is that Anatolia has always been a cradle where different identities can live together in an atmosphere of peace and tolerance. During the last few centuries Western societies have experienced the process which countries made up of multiple cultures must undergo, due to their expansion during the colonial period; in general they have come up against very serious issues in their adaptation to this new situation.

---

7 *See* John Freely, *Classical Turkey*, London; New York : Penguin Books, 1991; John Freely, *Türkiye Uygarlıklar Rehberi: Anadolu*, Istanbul: Yapı Kredi Yayınları, 2002.

8 For details *see* Benjamin Braude and Bernard Lewis (eds.), *Christians and Jews in the Ottoman Empire*, New York: Holmes-Meier Publishers, 1982.

Such issues are in fact still continuing in some places at present. Anatolia has had a multi-cultural experience throughout its history and has succeeded in carrying on this magnificent characteristic free of problems due to the fact that different cultures and religious traditions have been able to find safe havens for thousands of years.[9]

There is no doubt that the importance which the Islamic religion attaches to coexistence, the self-confidence inherent in being Muslim and to the enormous liberty that Islam recognizes for the followers of other religions have all had an important role in forming this legendary picture in Anatolia. As we witness the blood and tears shed in the name of peace in the Middle East, as we see the honor of humanity disregarded, human rights denigrated and efforts to thrust terror into the zone of religion, all things that have occurred during the last half century, we can only feel as human beings an exceptional longing for the experience of Anatolia. This experience, which indeed reflects human values in practice, and of which we have spoken so much, yet which we have somehow failed to put into practice, is very expressive in reality. For this reason, Anatolia's past and present accumulation, which reflects the understanding of coexistence without trying to make others as we are, which reflects an appreciation for others simply because they are human, without competition except to be kind and helpful, should inspire the rest of the world.

---

9 On the case of Jews in the Ottoman Empire and Modern Turkey *see* Avigdor Levy (ed.), *The Jews of the Ottoman Empire*, Princeton: Darwin Press, 1994; Stanford J. Shaw, *The Jews of the Ottoman Empire and the Turkish Republic*, London: The Macmillan Co., 1991; Walter F. Weiker, *Ottomans, Turks and the Jewish Polity: A History of the Jews of Turkey*, Lanham: University Press of America, Inc., 1992; Aryeh Shmuelevitz, *The Jews of the Ottoman Empire in the Late Fifteenth and the Sixteenth Centuries*, Leiden: E. J. Brill, 1984; Avigdor Levy (ed.), *Jews Turks Ottomans: A Shared History Fifteenth Through the Twentieth Century*, Syracuse: Syracuse University Press, 2002.

Freedom *with* Religion:
the Turkish Experience*

Human rights and freedom of religion Introduction

Although the freedom of religion is a fundamental human right, it is however one of the most debated rights, and is subject to conceptual objections as well as practical violations. This, perhaps, is due to disagreements about the nature of religion and its direct and indirect involvement in a broad range of subjects. For this reason, establishing a comprehensive set of rights to ensure the freedom of religion remains a challenge that is worth undertaking.[1]

There have been many attempts to define the freedom of religion in international legal agreements, such as "The Universal Declaration of Human Rights," and "The UN Declaration on the Elimination of All Forms of Intolerance and of Discrimination Based on Religion or Belief,"[2] and most recently, in the Constitution of the European Union. The way the freedom of religion is defined in these texts indicates that there is a close relationship between this freedom and freedom of conscience and thought.

---

* The full text of the paper was presented in a meeting on "Freedom of Religion in Christianity and Islam" organized by the Berlin Protestant Academy and the Berlin Catholic Academy in Berlin between 5-7 September 2004.

1 H. Robertson, *Human rights in the World: An Introduction to the Study of the International Protection of Human Rights*, Manchester: Manchester University, 1996; Michael J. Perry, *The Idea of Human Rights*, Oxford: Oxford University Press, 1998.

2 For these documents *see Twenty-five Human Rights Documents*, New York: Center for the Study of Human Rights, Columbia University, 2000.

However, it is clear that the scope of freedom of conscience and thought is wider than the scope of freedom of religion.[3]

The scope of the freedom of religion was broadly extended over the course of time. For instance, certain rights that were not stated explicitly in the Universal Declaration of Human Rights were later clarified and enumerated in subsequent texts, such as "the right of minorities to preserve their religion" and "the right of families to give their children religious and ethical education in accordance with their beliefs," and so on. These further additions and clarifications reveal that our understanding of religious freedom has developed in parallel with time and circumstances. Certain religious practices that were not considered to be within the scope of human rights today may possibly be included in this framework in the near future.[4]

In order to develop a sound framework for freedom of religion, it is necessary to understand the relevant concepts properly and to demonstrate the conceptual relations among them. In this sense, democracy, tolerance, pluralism, human will and human dignity are all seen to be closely related to freedom of religion. Some scholars claim that freedom of religion lies at the basis of all human rights. There are also those who argue that religious tolerance plays a dynamic role in the establishment of democratic societies.[5]

After this brief introduction, I will first refer to certain issues that are frequently associated with the freedom of religion in Islam.[6]

---

3 Ali Bardakoğlu. "Din ve Vicdan Hürriyeti: 2. Türk Hukukunda", *TDV Islam Ansiklopedisi*, c. 9, Istanbul: Isam, 1994, pp. 330-332.

4 Natan Lerner, *Religion, Beliefs and International Human Rights*, New York: Orbis Books, 2000; Tore Lindholm, W. Cole Durham and Bahia G. Tahzib-Lie (eds.), *Facilitating Freedom of Religion or Belief A Deskbook*, Leiden: Nijhoff, 2005.

5 For further discussion on this issue *see* Graham Maddox, *Religion and the Rise of Democracy*, London: Routledge, 1996; Larry Diamond, Marc F. Plattner, Philip J. Costopoulos (eds.), *World Religions and Democracy*, Baltimore: The Johns Hopkins University Press, 2005.

6 For general discussions on Islam and human rights *see* Ann Elizabeth Mayer, *Islam and*

Next, I will explain the historical roots and socio-cultural reasons for religious tolerance in Turkey. Finally, I will point to the main features of the Presidency of Religious Affairs in the context of state-religion relations. It will become clear that the experience of Turkey and the Presidency of Religious Affairs should be given particular attention, especially in the wake of recent developments in the world.

Islam and tolerance: There are certain basic principles that guarantee the freedom of religion in Islam. The foremost of these is the principle that religious belief must be based upon free choice. A well-known saying of the Prophet indicates that "religious deeds are considered according to the intentions." Thus, the belief of an individual is not acceptable if their intention was not pure and their faith was not sincere. Due to the close relation between faith and will, the Holy Qur'an clearly states that, "there is no compulsion in religion." (Al-Baqara 2: 256) The word "religion" in the verse implies the widest scope of this prohibition. It points to the inadmissibility of compelling anyone to adopt any religion in general.

The Qur'an justifies this prohibition by indicating that right and wrong, truth and falsehood are explicitly obvious. Thus, it is up to the individual to use their mental faculties to make a choice among alternatives. Where no alternative is provided then the sincerity of the individual's choice is questionable.[7]

The principle of pluralism: Another principle that guarantees the freedom of religion in Islam is the fact that Divine Will is not aimed at gathering all of humanity under one religion. The Qur'an addresses the Prophet, saying: "And if thy Lord willed, all who are in the earth would have believed together. Wouldst thou

---

Human Rights: Tradition and Politics, 2nd ed. Boulder: Westview Press, 1995; Shaikh Shaukat Hussain, *Human rights in Islam,* New Delhi: Kitab Bhavan, 1990.

7 Khaled Abou El-Fadl, "The place of Tolerance in Islam: On reading the Qur'an and misreading it", *Boston Review,* Dec. 2001-Jan. 2002, pp. 24-51.

(Muhammad) compel men until they are believers?" (Yunus 10:99). In a different verse, the importance of individual preference is indicated, confirming that: "so let he who will believe, and let he who will disbelieve" (Al-Kahf 18:29). This verse, though not approving disbelief, allocates high priority to the will of the individual, stating that they should be free in choosing their religion, an extremely important issue. These verses confirm that human beings have always followed different religious beliefs and practices throughout history, while suggesting that these differences will possibly persist in the future. There is no doubt that ignoring this fact would cause serious violations in the area of religious freedom.[8]

The principle of reciprocity: The principle of reciprocity is one of the most basic ethical and legal principles in Islam and it can be observed in various forms. For example, good deeds are rewarded in this world and in the world to come, economic and social agreements or contracts should be honored, and in ethics, "do unto others as you would have them do unto you." The principle of reciprocity is also indicated in the Qur'an with respect to the freedom of religion. In the face of the difficulties and cruelties to which the Prophet was subjected, God asked him to respond by quoting the following verse: "You shall have your religion and I shall have my religion." (Al-Kafiroon 109:6) A further example based on the principle of reciprocity that guarantees the freedom of religion in Islam is associated with the prohibition of blasphemy. The Qur'an prohibits Muslims from uttering swear words against "the gods" of other religions: "And do not abuse those whom they call upon besides, lest exceeding the limits they should abuse Allah out of ignorance. Thus have We made fair seeming to every people their deeds; then to their Lord shall be their return, so He will inform them of what they did." (Al-An'am 6:108).

---

8 David George Mullan (ed.), *Religious Pluralism in The West: An Anthology*, Massachusetts: Blackwell Publishers, 1998; Leif Manger (ed.), *Muslim Diversity: Local Islam in Global Context*, London: Curzon Press, 1999.

Prejudices and issues

In spite of the principles that secure the freedom of religion in Islam, we are encountering some harmful tendencies at present in some Muslim and non-Muslim countries. Such tendencies have come to the fore particularly in the wake of September 11. Unfortunately, some people who have resorted to violence claim that they are acting in the name of Islam.[9] Nothing can be further from the truth. Islam is the religion of peace and it equates the killing of an innocent person with the killing of all human beings. We also have observed that there are some people in the West who intentionally associate Islam with violence and terror. Today, Muslims are faced by two arduous tasks: They have to combat the extremists among themselves, and they have to correct the negative image of Islam that has been fed intentionally and malignantly to various circles. There is a great need for dialogue and cooperation between Muslims and people of common sense in the West. In order to transform the reciprocal mistrust into confidence and cooperation, each side has responsibilities. As a first step, to eliminate mutual prejudice and to install a healthy process of understanding and dialogue, each side has to avoid name-calling and take the utmost care to be respectful, particularly when talking about the other.

An example of the negative image formation that is going on is the use of adjectives inserted in front of the word "Islam"; these words go against the spirit of the religion, its historical experience and its present position. Among these adjectives are "moderate Islam", "radical Islam", "fundamentalist Islam," etc. It is important to see what is being implied by the use of these adjectives. Is it pos-

---

9 On the impact of 9/11 *see* Verna V. Gehring (ed.), *War after September 11*, Lanham: Rowman & Littlefield Publishing, 2003; Ian Markham and Ibrahim M. Abu-Rabi (eds.) *11 September: Religious Perspectives on the Causes and Consequences*, Oxford: Oneworld Publications, 2002; Bruce Lincoln, *Holy Terrors: Thinking About Religion After September 11*, Chicago: The University of Chicago Press, 2003.

sible to say that there are various Islams, one being moderate, one radical, one extremist? No. We believe that all Divine religions are moderate and that they are the source of peace and harmony. Nevertheless, we admit that there is moderation and extremism in every religion. We cannot ignore the fact that religion is exploited in various parts of the world by extreme movements and tendencies. Therefore, one must not define a religion by merely looking at the behavior of (some of) its followers. A scholarly and ethical attitude requires giving priority to how the religion defines itself. Islam characterizes itself as a religion of peace[10] that denounces all kinds of extremism.[11]

Jihad: In recent years, some Western writers have made frequent references to the concept of *jihad*, presenting it as being opposed to the freedoms of religion and conscience. It is important to note that the term *jihad* is different from the term used for "war" *(harb)* or "battle" *(qital)* in Arabic. The primary meaning of *jihad* is to make one's best effort or to struggle. When the verses that contain the word *jihad* are interpreted with the primary meaning of the term, they indicate that Muslims have to make every effort to perform deeds that please God and receive His approval. That is why the term *major jihad* in the sayings of the Prophet refers to the struggle between a person and his conscience. Islam is entirely unfamiliar with the term "holy war". War has never been characterized, by any means whatsoever, as holy in Islam. Wars may or may not happen; in any given situation a war may be legitimate due to certain reasons or not legitimate due to others. The Qur'an did not, at any time whatsoever, consider a continuous and limitless war as legitimate. According to the principle of reciprocity, the Qur'an indicates that Muslims had to fight those who fight them. (al-Baqara 2:191). Yet, even in this situation, the Qur'an prohibits

---

10 *See* Nasri Salhab, *Islam as I came to Know It, A Religion of Mercy and Peace*, Translated by Ali Azeriah, Rabat: ISESCO, 2001,

11 On the issue of representing a negative image of Islam *see* Edward W. Said, *Covering Islam*, New York: Pantheon Books, 1981.

Muslims from "exceeding the limits" (al-Baqara 2:190 and Al-Maeda 5:2).

It is important to keep in mind that the Qur'an gives priority to peace and demands that Muslims "enter into a state of peace altogether" (al-Bakara 2:208). "And if they incline to peace, then incline to it and trust in Allah; surely He is the Hearing, the Knowing" (al-Anfal 8:61). In another verse, the Qur'an says, "Therefore if they withdraw from you and do not fight you and offer you peace, then Allah has not given you a way against them" (an-Nisa 4:90). All these verses clearly show that Islam is a religion of peace; it prefers and exalts peace over war.[12]

Terror: Terror is another concept that is sometimes unjustly associated with Islam or Muslims. Here again there is a misconception and misrepresentation. The Qur'an not only disapproves of terror, but also openly condemns it by defining it as something that supports defeatism in the world. Bloodshed, egoism, injustice and terror may be tendencies that are concealed in human nature. These tendencies may be controlled with arts and education, religion and morals, laws and sanctions that provide social order, that is to say, with the assistance of the elements that constitute human civilization. Violence and terror do not stem from religion. The Islamic world, as well as the West, should question themselves about what the motives of the existing violence are. Should the vast gap that exists at present between the underdeveloped and developed countries persist? What are the reasons behind the increment of terror and violence in the shadow of globalization and modernity?

Religious inclinations that are not under the control of sound and trustworthy religious knowledge have created problems in the past and will continue to do so today. If such knowledge and under-

---

12 For historical experience of social and religious peace *see* Ekmeleddin İhsanoğlu, *A Culture of Peaceful Coexistence: Early Islamic and Ottoman Turkish Examples*, Istanbul: IRCICA, 2004.

standing had not been produced, styles of pathologic religiosity would have been introduced. If this had been the case, then sentiments would dominate reason, and individual desires, as well as regional differences, would gather strength under the name of religion; in this case, the features that threaten peace and tranquility would assume a sacred appearance. It is obvious that religious affiliation, race, ethnic identity and regional identity can be easily channeled into violence in societies where irrational emotions and devotion are present instead of rational thinking and sound knowledge. Where the distribution of economic income creates vast inequalities and where underemployment exist alongside concerns for the future the same problems will persist. In dealing with the ailments of the human conundrum, it is important to analyze the problem properly and not to yield to easy and superficial explanations. Here as well, we need to resist prejudices and search for ways of cooperation in order to eradicate this problem together.

The Ottoman heritage in the context of freedom of religion

When Turkey is compared with other Islamic countries, we observe that there exists a positive atmosphere with respect to the freedom of religion. This is because the religious understanding and practice in Turkey is molded by Islamic tradition and historical experience. In our tradition, there are spiritual guides in the area of religious freedom and tolerance such as Rumi, Yunus Emre and Haci Bektaş Veli, all of who conveyed a message of peace and love to all of humanity. These spiritual leaders were the products of the culture of tolerance that was created in Anatolia over the millennia.

The Ottoman State ruled over three continents and its borders extended from the Balkans to the Caucasus and from the Middle East to North Africa between the 13th and the 20th centuries.[13] There were more than twenty ethnic communities living in the

---

13 Leon Carl Brown (ed.), *Imperial Legacy: the Ottoman Imprint on the Balkans and the Middle East*, New York: Columbia University Press, 1996.

Ottoman lands, speaking dozens of languages. Christianity and Judaism, with their various sects and denominations, were the most prevalent religions after Islam in the Ottoman State.

The Ottoman State ruled these religious groups through a "Millet System." The non-Muslims were subject to Islamic jurisprudence in matters pertaining to public order, while they were subject to their own religious jurisdiction in matters related to civil law, law of inheritance and commerce. This system ensured the establishment of a just administration that did not discriminate among religions, languages, races, or colors. The ratio of non-Muslims to Muslims in the Ottoman Empire between 1500 and 1850 was nearly 40% to 60%. This ratio alone shows that "the Ottoman Peace" was a real success.[14]

The Turkish experience: Law and the freedom of religion

The Ottoman Empire was gradually transformed from the millet system[15] into the constitutional state, and certain legal developments took place in the field of freedom of religion. For instance, the Constitution of 1876 recognized the freedom of worship for religious minorities. The Constitution of 1909 reinstated the same rights for all. With the establishment of the Turkish Republic, certain changes, such as the abolishment of the Caliphate and the unification of education further cleared the way for the project of secularization. The Constitution of 1924 characterized freedom of conscience (religion) as a natural right for every citizen. With the constitutional amendments of 1937, it was stated that secularism was one of the basic principles of the Republic.

---

14 Nesimi Yazici. "Osmanlılarda Bir arada Yaşama Tecrübesi ve Dini Müsamaha Üzerine Bazı Mülahazalar", *Uluslararası Avrupa Birliği Şurası: Tebliğ ve Müzakereleri (3-7 Mayıs 2000), c. II*. Ankara: Diyanet İşleri Başkanlığı Yayınları, 2000, pp. 522-536.

15 On the millet system *see* M. Macit Kenanoğlu, *Osmanlı Millet Sistemi: Mit ve Gerçek*, Istanbul: Klasik, 2004; Bilal Eryılmaz, *Osmanlı Devletinde Millet Sistemi*, Istanbul: Ağaç Yayıncılık, 1992.

The Constitution of 1961 reaffirmed the freedom of conscience, religious belief and conviction including the right for free worship and religious rituals. The Constitution of 1982 preserved the contents of this Constitution. In addition to these constitutional developments that protected the freedom of religion, Turkey also ratified the Universal Declaration of Human Rights in 1954 and adopted the articles pertaining to the freedom of religion mentioned in the declaration.[16]

As these developments show, the Turkish Republic has a secular system that is similar to those of Western countries. It could even be argued that as secularism has been taken as a basic principle of the state and that no reference is made to Islam in its constitution, the Turkish Republic is more secular than the European countries that accept Christianity as the state religion or do not openly refer to secularism in their constitutions.

Sometimes the stability of Turkey's secular system is questioned. We should not forget that secularism is deeply rooted in Turkish society and it is not possible to change direction in a country like Turkey that has been progressing towards modernization for the last two centuries. Muslims in Turkey have internalized modernization. The six centuries of the Ottoman experience show that the Turkish people know how to maintain the balance between religion and state. Turkey's experiences constitute a very special case among Muslim countries.

The Presidency of Religious Affairs and freedom of religion

Although the Presidency of Religious Affairs *(Diyanet İşleri*

---

16 On the deveoplment of secularism in Turkey *see* B. Lewis*The Emergence of Modern Turkey*, London: Oxford University Press, 1961; Şerif Mardin, 'Religion and Secularism in Turkey' in A. Kazancigil and E. Ozbudun (eds.) *Atatürk: Founder of a Modern Turkey*, London: C. Hurst and Company, 1981, pp. 191-219; Şerif Mardin, 'Religion and Politics in Modern Turkey' in James A. Piscatori (ed.) *Islam in the Political Process*, Cambridge: Cambridge University Press, 1988, pp. 138-159; Niyazi Berkes, *The Development of Secularism in Turkey*, Introduction by Feroz Ahmad, London: Hurst & Company, 1998.

Başkanlığı) is historically related to the institution of Sheikh-ul-Islam in the Ottoman State, it is not a continuation of the same institution. There are substantial differences between them from the point of view of purpose and function. The duties and authorities of the institution of Şeyhülislamlık in the Ottoman State ranged from religious jurisdiction and education to religious services. With the establishment of the Republic, some of these duties were relegated to other institutions. The Presidency of Religious Affairs was established as an institution in harmony with the secular structure of the state and was charged with the duty of enlightening the community with religious matters as well as administering religious services and the functioning of places of worship.

The Diyanet, in classical religious literature, is used in opposition to the judiciary. The judiciary is concerned with legal, political and administrative relationships among individuals and with the process of imposing legal sanctions by public institutions; the Diyanet has a different meaning. It refers to the spiritual and moral aspects of the individual and to the consistency of their internal conscience. For this reason, allocating the name of the Diyanet to this institution during the era of the Republic could be interpreted as a sign that the project was aimed at basing itself on religiosity from an ethical axis.

The reason for the existence of the Presidency proceeds from the needs of the people in the field of religious matters and from their requests for religious services. Thus, the Presidency was established in order to meet these needs and requests. The Presidency is one of the constitutional organizations of the Turkish Republic. Consequently, it has to fulfill all of its activities in accordance with the authority given to it by the Constitution and in accordance with the laws and regulations. The Presidency represents neither a group nor a religious community, and it is not in any way an alternative for such communities. The Presidency as a superior organization is an institution that provides its services to all individuals. Although

the Presidency is a public institution, it does not operate along political lines; it fulfills its services with the perceptiveness of the public laws and order.

The basic duty of the Presidency is to provide its services to
people according to the common denominator of Islam. Individuals
may possibly add to this their own inclinations, preferences and
their religious understandings. At this stage, the Presidency does
not aim to reduce such differences or to equalize them, but endeavors to submit reliable religious information to individuals in this
subject. For this reason, it would also be incorrect to define the
Diyanet as a Sunni institution. The Presidency aims at embracing
all people who qualify themselves as Muslim; it is an institution
that endeavors at all times to enlighten and acknowledge each individual, whether that person goes to the mosque or not, or worships
or not.

There are three basic characteristics for the Presidency as a public institution. First, it is a public institution; it provides its services
within the framework of the Constitution and the laws. Second, it is
a free institution; it puts a special emphasis on producing religious
knowledge in a free atmosphere. Third, it is a civil organization;
that is to say, it takes seriously the accumulated religious experiences of the people and their requests, and it provides the most suitable services for them. Due to these three characteristics, as a constitutional, free, and civil organization, the Presidency is able to
function and serve in harmony with the secular principles and
implications of the freedom of religion.

The Presidency also sends its personnel to serve Turkish immi-
grant communities in Europe.[17] For this purpose, the Presidency has

---

17 On Turkish communities in Europe *see* B. Beeley, *Migration, The Turkish Case*, Third
World Studies, Case Study 8, Milton Keynes: The Open University Press, 1983; P. L.
Martin, *The Unfinished Story: Turkish Labour Migration to Western Europe*, Geneva: International Labour Office, 1991; Talip Küçükcan, *Politics of Ethnicity, Identity and Religion: Turkish-Muslims in Britain*, Avebury: Ashgate, 1999.

established special programs to train its personnel in the language and culture of the country where they will serve. It is important that these personnel are cognizant and competent in the field of religious services and careful to prevent harmful religious trends. They are expected to contribute effectively in the process of developing and generalizing a sound religious understanding among the Muslims who live in Europe. They must also be aware of the deeds that might be considered as "abuses of freedom".

We are obliged to bring about improvement, transformation, progress and modernization with the help of a sound moral and religious line. For this reason, the Presidency of Religious Affairs lays the ground for interpreting Islam in accordance with the needs and values of the present century, giving priority to the basic principles of religion, and making good use of the traditions. It is at this point that our Presidency provides an important service that might be called "freedom *with* religion."

Religion, Change and Modern Life*

When discussing the topic of "religion, change and modern life", it is essential that we discuss the nature of religion, as well as the relevancy of religion to the individual and society.[1] This is of particular importance in the case of Islam, as it has strong forms of advice and rules concerning human behavior with regard to belief, worship and moral life. On the other hand, the relationship of Islam with social change and modern life, the influence of Islam on these or the shape that Islam gives to these are closely related with the universality and continuity of religion.

Since general and personal rulings that are related to the practical life of Islam exist in the main religious texts and also as a rational fact that is related to the historical circumstances and flow of life, these rulings have been placed in the center of religious arguments, particularly during times when serious social changes have taken place. On the way to this phase, the methodological arguments which deal with how religious rulings are to be understood and interpreted according to time and place, in other words, the method of *ijtihad* (the process of making legal decisions) used to establish the relationship between the main sources of the religion and events, has gained a distinct importance. The increasing occurrences of *ijtihad* and calls made for it during encounters with for-

---

* This paper was presented at the International Conference entitled "Islam and Modern Society in Turkey" organized by the Konrad Adenauer Foundation and the Goethe Institute in Istanbul on 22-23 November 2004.
1 On religion and social change *see* David Herbert (ed.), *Religion and Social Transformations: Religion Today, Tradition, Modernity and Change*, Milton Keynes: Ashgate, 2002; David L. Edwards, *Religion and Change*, London: Hodder and Stoughton, 1969.

eign cultures after the conquests or invasions in Islamic history were directly caused by those ascending voices that were looking for change.[2]

In order to comprehend truly what sort of relation exists between Islam and the modern life in which we live, it is necessary to focus upon *ijtihad* and introduce a discussion about the function it undertakes and even about its true nature; *ijtihad* means the interpretation of religious texts and the updating of them in such a way that they will be appropriate to everyday life.[3]

Here it would be useful to touch upon the ongoing discussions and concerns that are centered on the concepts of modernism, modernity, tradition and change in the Muslim world over the last few centuries.

1. When looking at religion from the perspective that religions all emanate from a common line descending from the prophets, we realize that religions explain the celestial/metaphysical life in the physical world in which we live and represent the immutability of this world. The essence of the Divine message that began with Adam and continued with Abraham, Moses and Jesus, finally coming to an end with Mohammed, transmits the Divine wisdom of actuality and the presentation of the perspective of creation, indicating the importance of eternal life. The emphasis that is frequently made in the Qur'an that this message has been inherited from the prophets, the information that is given concerning the creation, as well as the beginning and the end of existence, the basic fundamentals of belief, the principles of worship and morals are all clear

---

2 Here it is useful to recall the efforts of the expounders of Islamic laws who played a leading role in the establishment of the schools of law during the time when the Islamic geography was expanding rapidly in the second and third century after the migration, the Mongolian invasion and the Crusades, up until the meeting up with the West in the last century, as well as recalling their ideas like public interest (*maslaha*), objectives (*makasid*), renovation (*tajdid*), *ijtihad* and the reconstruction of religious thought.

3 On the concept of ijtihad *see* Imran Ahsan Khan Nyazee, *Theories of Islamic Law: The Methodology of Ijtihad*, Kuala Lumpur: Other Press, 2002.

signs of the immutable line of divine religion. Although perceptions vary according to the level of consciousness and thought of the person addressed, there is continuity in the ideas contained in the divine texts. Religion has the function of supporting, testing, establishing and protecting the original aspects of human kind by preserving instinct and sanity. The human being has been sent to the world and placed in a highly esteemed and superior position, while at the same time they have been created with some weaknesses. It is because of this that people live, whether in mind or action, with good and evil, with justice and cruelty, mercy and mercilessness, altruism and egoism. The first of these merely represents the fundamental line directed by reason and nature, while the second signifies the accidental line that is created by the physical and bodily world. Religion, which confirms the first line, supports human beings and guides them by lighting their way so that they can continue without surrendering to weakness or deviation. For this reason, the revelation sent through the prophets is indeed a boundless blessing and is a form of assistance for human beings who were created by God and sent to the world with free will and the ability to perform whatever action they wish.

2. As a general rule, it is true that the social relations of humanity have undergone continuous and significant changes throughout history. Yet, when this is looked at from a distance, we can realize that humanity has undergone these changes in a limited area that is surrounded by possibilities and impossibilities. In spite of the ineffectiveness and indispensability of such great changes, we can observe that the main line, with relation to the fundamental characteristics of human beings, has been protected. Those who carefully observe the adventure of human life will realize that despite the changes that have been experienced in modern life in the field of law and the social and political structure, and also in spite of all the changes that will be realized, certain merits and principles have been protected in the field of law and fundamental human behavior.

Perceiving the distinction between those two fields, and understanding how the relationship in each field has been established by religion will be important in adding more depth to the argument concerning religion, renovation and social change. Fundamentally, it would not be correct at this point to introduce the experience of religion and humanity as alternatives or rivals to one another. On the contrary, they must be described as two separate entities that are fed from the same source. Therefore, it would be erroneous to think that the rules and types of behavior that form part of humanity's experience and which are the reflection of social change as being entirely opposed to the Divine will or as entirely independent from the Divine source.

3. Belief represents the fundamentals of faith, which implies recognizing and loving the Almighty, and the act of worship, which means devotion to Him according to certain symbolic behavior, according to His wishes. Belief and worship together constitute the center of Islam. Since the fundamentals of belief and acts of worship have also been determined through religious revelations, they are not open to change or modernization. On the contrary, their meaning and effect will last for as long as they are carried out. This is true for all religions. Here, it is important not to break away from the original discipline of the same religion and to try hard to understand other religions, instead of judging them. Although the teachings of a religion that are related to individual and social ethics, from the point of view of the basic moral and human values on which the religion is based, hold universality and permanence, there is a need that they should be expressed in a new way that is in step with social changes, and which shows that these teachings are closely connected to local circumstances. Because such a separation is possible in the field of law, where a social and moral consensus can transform the norms supported by the public, it is here that the subject of permanency and change should be analyzed.

4. The teachings of the main sources of Islam have closely influ-

enced the tradition of Muslim societies, their culture and civilization, the family structure, individual and social lives, and have even played an important role in shaping these factors throughout history. Nevertheless, new interpretations of these teachings have reflected certain differences according to the times when they came out and the prevailing circumstances that were present. As a result, there have been reciprocal influences. There is no doubt that such a process has occurred in spite of the resistance of Islam against change. On the contrary, Islam has left the door open for such flexible influences deliberately so that its universality and vividness can continue at all times. It is for this reason that Islam has attached great importance to reason, understanding, interpretation, individual initiative and responsibility in religion. It is because of these circumstances that the message brought by Islam, the principles upon which it has placed importance, the objectives it has demonstrated and the examples and clarifications it has indicated, have been analyzed since the early period of Islam in a methodical way. Again, as a result of such analysis, the judgments that are related to the individual and social life of Islam have been seen as differing from behavior patterns and models, as well as being different with respect to the principles carried in its essence and the objectives fostered.

As a result, religious sciences that have been established and developed by Muslims, in particular the science of the methodology of law, have opened a well-traveled road. It is in this way that the main teachings of religious disciplines have been able to continue without being shaken, while still introducing the tradition of interpretation that was formed around this discipline. Thus, the precedent was set for making new interpretations according to new circumstances on methodological foundations. During the periods of cultural unrest that were faced by the Islamic world, calls were made and effort expended to bring about change; this change was always aimed at questioning and weeding out what was tradition without disrupting the essence of the religion.

5. The traditional view of Islamic scholars in the classical period was that the events and the rulings found in religious texts were limited, while the events encountered by individuals are limitless. There was also agreement that religious texts can encompass limitless events, if interpretation and reasoning are used. However, in the view of the scholars, introducing religious judgments is the responsibility of God, and *ijtihad* (interpretation) does not mean introducing new judgments, but rather means demonstrating the extent of the existing texts. In other words, the Islamic scholars of the classical period were convinced that *ijtihad* only played the role of exploring and revealing the extent of religious judgments.

If religious judgments then are norms that have direct relationships with religion and which are clearly specified by the Qur'an and the Sunna, and if *ijtihad* is an activity that is aimed at understanding these norms, then theories that focus on the words that equate *ijtihad* with analogy (*qiyas*) become more meaningful, and interpretation becomes an explorative activity whereby one is able to understand religious judgments. In this event, the interpretation that is carried out by religious scholars, and which literally means the understanding and clarifying of religious texts, becomes limited to a narrow field, whereas other subjects become part of a wide field of interpretation and are left open to the initiative of the individual and society. Thus, previously social change did not greatly influence religious interpretation, while the second type of *ijtihad* was affected by the actors of change.

If what is meant by religious judgments is all types and patterns of behavior produced from direct or indirect expositions of the Qur'an and the Sunna as well as from the secondary elements that have been mentioned, that is to say, all the rules and regulations that have are part of the practical life of Muslims, both individuals and society, and if these are all presented as areas in which the legislator, in the classical connotation, can operate, then a heavy burden has been thrown upon the shoulders of scholars and the religion alike. It is without a doubt that the experience of humanity, which can become contaminated during the natural flow mentioned above, must be tested and controlled from the perspective of religious discipline. This, in fact, would be a useful and beneficial method to prevent deviations that go against the principles of religion. However, this procedure may open the door to difficulties, as there will be attempts to find the answer to every event in religion and there is a chance that we may become mired down in the explanations of religious scholars. Moreover, steps that may be taken without determining directly or indirectly the area of interest of the religion in this subject, or without determining the historical experience of Muslims in relation to religion, will weaken the reliability of religious scholars and will make the general acceptance of religion difficult, as well as lessening the authority of the religion in the conscience of the people.

6. The extent to which religion has been influenced by social change has always been a subject of lively debate, not only from the perspective of Islam, but also for other religions. The acceptance of Christianity by the Roman Empire in the fourth century was something that would be discussed by social scientists hundreds of years later. Did Rome influence Christianity or Christianity Rome? This is in fact a didactic question, as religion not only influences life, but is also influenced by life.

It is a scientific and historical fact that religious concepts influence social life and that these concepts are influenced by the lifestyle of the society. This fact is clearly displayed in the example of Rome and Christianity. There is no doubt that all parts of our life are not independent from each other, which is why art and architecture reflect, for example, the developments that take place in social and religious spheres. We can trace the same phenomenon in the economy. Weber, one of the founders of sociology, demonstrates the influence of religion on very different spheres, like the economy, in his famous work *The Ethics of Protestantism and the Spirit of Capitalism.*

7. Religion, Tradition and Modern Society: I believe that the whole problem of reform and modern life emerges from an insufficient appreciation of the reciprocal influence that exists between the life-styles of societies and religious concepts or from an inadequate comprehension of the fact that not only does religion regulate the life-style of society, but also that religion itself has been greatly influenced by society.

The concept of "tradition", which is usually used as being synonymous with religion, is the most fundamental notion we face regarding the relationship between religion and modernity. This is valid not only for the Islamic world, but for other religions as well. Currently, the different opinions of some Islamic scholars are important in revealing how we should perceive tradition; some consider that tradition has a normative character and they seek rationality and change in it, while others insist that while we should not neglect tradition, it is also necessary to take the human experience into consideration as well.[4] Yet tradition is nothing more than an accumulation that has come about as a result of the interpretations of our ancestors to the unchangeable sacred truth established by religion at the beginning. There is no doubt that this accumulation contains useful elements and tenets. Yet, it is possible that those who shaped the tradition in the past could have been mistaken, just like us, or they could have made those interpretations according to their own time, geography and needs.

If we consider tradition to be a phenomenon that has useful terms but that does not have to be accepted as a whole, then we can see that it is not necessary to build a barrier between modernity and tradition; they can both exist side by side. Moreover, there are many things that modernity can gain from tradition, and vice versa. For example, tradition can be of use to people today with the humanist

---

4 Mehmet S. Aydın, "Rational Thought and Islamic Modernism", paper presented at the Symposium of Islamic Thought, Istanbul, 1995.

values and merits it contains to help the individual surpass the cold structure of modernity that gives prominence to individualism which in turn paves the way to isolation. The concept of transpersonal psychology, which is being discussed more and more in the West today, is nothing less than inviting religious tradition to help. Today, the entire world, in particular the West, has discovered that religion has a positive potential to find solutions for a multitude of social problems. At the other end of the spectrum, modernity can assist with its rational perspective in cleansing tradition of elements that are contradictory to the essence of religion. During the process of mutual assistance, it is essential that tradition is not transformed into traditionalism or modernity into modernism.

Modernism or modernity: It is undeniable that modern production has been successful in reaching entire cultures and geographies and in bringing out new merits, whether good or bad, in a world where globalization has eliminated frontiers. Nevertheless, all societies still preserve their cultural and traditional forms. Today, the duty of societies that have been influenced by Western cultures, like those of the Muslim world, has forced them to struggle to transform these traditional forms without deviating from the essence of religion, while still taking the conditions of today into consideration. This does not mean that the contents of reform that have taken place in the West or the demands of the modern world that contradict the essence of religion should be ratified by religion or by religious institutions. Unfortunately, such suggestions are quite often perceived as demands for a "reform" that will shake the foundation of the religion, and those who make such proposals are seen to be a Martin Luther,[5] reading the ninety-nine articles of his reform movement from his horse in front of Wittenberg University.

Three hundred years ago religion put science into a place it did

---

5 Martin Luther, *Martin Luther's Basic Theological Writings, 1483-1546;* edited by Timothy F. Lull; foreword by Jaroslav Pelikan, Minneapolis: Fortress Press, 1989.

not deserve to be in. Today, religion has been forced to share the same fate by modernization. Yet, there is no justification for the perception that "anything that is a modern thing is absolutely opposed to religion and in particular to Islam". Islam approaches no thought with prejudice; on the contrary, it can live harmoniously with any elements that are not opposed to its basic criteria. Moreover, Islam does not allege that it is a religion of a specific time or geography, but rather claims that it is valid for all times and geographies.

It is true that the Enlightenment caused a sharp decline in religious life in the West.[6] Nevertheless, the idea of the Enlightenment had positive affects in two areas. The first understanding represents the positivist idea, or the Enlightenment movement of the atheists. The second perception represents the idea that claims science is a factor that develops and enlightens the human conscious while transforming us into a form that encourages us to embrace religion. This perception has led to a situation today in the West, and particularly in the United States of America, the most industrial, technological, and modern country in the world, where 70 per cent of the citizens define themselves as religious. Research carried out in this country proves that the percentage of people who believe in God has never fallen below 90%.[7] It is clear that people have taken on some of the positive aspects of the Enlightenment while also protecting their religious identities. In addition, they do not feel obliged to adopt all the ideas and values of the Enlightenment.

---

6 On the impact of Enlightenment on religion *see* James E. Bradley and Dale K. Van Kley (eds.), *Religion and Politics in Enlightenment Europe*, Notre Dame: University of Notre Dame, 2001; Norman Hampson, *The Enlightenment,* London: Penguin Books, 1990; R. Rémond, *Religion and Society in Modern Europe*, Oxford: Blackwell Publishers, 1999.

7 Ali Köse, "New Paradigms on the Relations of Modernity and Secularization", *Liberal Thought* , Spring 2001, vol. 24, pp.150-165; Robert Booth Fowler, Allen D. Hertzke, Laura R. Olson, *Religion and politics in America: faith, culture, and strategic choices*, Boulder: Westview Press, 1999; Peter W. Williams (ed.), *Perspectives on American Religion and Culture* , Oxford: Blackwell Publishers, 1999.

Here, the main point to be taken into consideration is to determine whether the religious characters of the Enlightenment are automatically equivalent to the process of modernization. If modernization is the same as the Enlightenment, then it is not possible that those who believe in the importance of religious values have accepted this. Here, we must redefine terms. The Enlightenment is an ideology, and this ideology aims at materializing social change under the umbrella of modernism. In fact, modernity is no more than a situation, a phenomenon that is experienced. It consists of the problems, the demands and the solutions of the age that have been brought before you. Yet, it is possible to enrich these problems and demands with new formulas; you can take what you want and get rid of what you want. In order to do this, you must have your own formulas and your values must be genuine and applicable. Thus, the relationship of the Islamic world to modernity and the idea that "one can be religious while being modern" should be evaluated against this background. Those who express such an idea generally believe that Islam is universal and above time and this is why Islam is a religion that is easily followed in every age. The values that are deemed at present as the values of this age, such as religious freedom, rational thinking, democracy, equality, rights of woman, and similar ideas, are in fact values of Islam. This is something that is accepted even by the most extreme members of the Islamic world. A Muslim who denies the above cannot be acquainted with the Farewell Speech delivered by Prophet Muhammad.

Will Islam face the fate of the church in the Enlightenment? The Church did not know what to do when it came up against the pressure of the Enlightenment. First, it opposed this movement, and then removed itself, closing its windows on the outside world. But it could not maintain this stance for long and was compelled to open its windows, little by little in self-defense. The Church then gave permission to those elements and demands that it considered to be harmless or not of great danger. Yet, by this time the windows were wide open, so wide that they could not be closed again. In 1962 the Second Vatican Council[8] gave signals that implied that the Vatican had gone down a road from which it could no longer return, due to the basic concept with which the Council had been recognized (*aggiornamento*); the Church was now encouraged to conform to the modern world. The Church, at last, was forced to give up, having abandoned its principles and it had become helpless. The Church hoisted the white flag; it surrendered to the extent that today it no longer considers homosexuality to be a sin, and it has even turned a blind eye to homosexual priests. As a result, the Church has lost its creditability with devout Christians; they were confronted with a Church that tolerated all the demands of the modern world and which issued advisory opinions in accordance with these demands.

Whether the experiences of the Church in the West after its contact with modernity and the process of surrendering are valid for the Muslim world or not is one of the most important issues that faces the Islamic world at present. This is why we must decide what to do concerning this issue as soon as possible. There are three ways to do this: the first is to close the windows firmly, as the Church did at the beginning and to assume that no such thing as modernity exists, behaving as if it will not influence us as long as we refuse to acknowledge it. The second thing we can do is what the Church does today in the West; that is to surrender and give in to all the demands of the modern world. The third is to determine a road map that will enable us to evaluate and compare the demands of the modern world with our authentic religious criteria that have not been diluted with traditional beliefs.

Multiple modernity and Islam: I think that the majority of Muslims will embrace the third choice. The prerequisites for bring-

---

8 For a detailed discussion *see* G.C. Berkouwer, *The Second Vatican Council and the New Catholicism*, translated by Lewis B. Smedes, Michigan: William B. Eerdmans Publishing Company, 1965; Hans Küng, *The Living Church: Reflections on the Second Vatican Council*, translated by Cecily Hastings, N. D. Smith, London: Sheed and Ward, 1963.

ing this about are that first we must behave in a realistic manner and then we must be self-confident. The most important principle of the former is to admit that interaction is unavoidable, that cultural contact is indispensable and globalization is an undeniable fact of this world. The most significant principle of the latter is that one should be confident when developing a culture without compromising one's religion.

Being modern does not mean undergoing the same process of enlightenment that the West did, or admitting the values that have been imposed by this process at the expense of one's religious and cultural merits. Today a new concept emerges from the sociology of religion under the name of "multiple modernity"[9] This new concept argues that modernity is not the privilege of only one culture or geography, that is to say cultures outside the West can and will develop their own modernity. The sociologist Peter Berger is among those who defend this new approach; in particular he draws attention to the fact that the modern Turkish Muslim who lives in urban areas feels themselves to be more religious than their fellow Muslims who live in rural areas. Berger makes the same point for Indonesia as well.[10] Rodney Stark, another sociologist, draws attention to the fact that the research carried out in different regions of the world reveals that the religiosity level of Muslims has increased with modernity.[11] The findings of Joseph Tamney, known for his research on the Muslims of Java, demonstrate that Islamic practices increase with modernity. He argues that Islam, with its flexible structure, is talented at adapting itself against the threats of modernity.[12]

---

9 Samuel N. Eisenstadt, *Multiple Modernities*, Transaction Publishers, 2002 ; Aziz Azmeh, *Islams and Modernities*, London: Verso, 1993.
10 Peter L. Berger, "Secularism in Retreat", *National Interest*, Winter 1996/97, vol.5, pp.3-12.
11 Rodney Stark, "Secularization: R.I.P." in *The Secularization Debate;* William H. Swatos & Daniel V. Olson (eds.), New York, Rowman & Littelfield, 2000, pp. 44-66.
12 Joseph B. Tamney, "Fasting and Modernization", *Journal for the Scientific Study of Religion*, 1980, Vol. 19, pp. 129-37.

The main point that needs to be clarified in our minds is that modernity is not equivalent to being this-worldly, in other words, modernity does not mean abstracting the individual from the values and influence of religion or compelling them to establish a life style with no religion. Thus, modernity is not an instrument that brings an altogether worldly life without religion. No doubt this was the aim of the Enlightenment process at the beginning, as it was believed that the life of this world, which emerged as a result of modernity, would erase religion from the Earth.[13] Yet, as has been clearly articulated by many sociologists in the West, modernity rescued itself from being the forerunner of the "Positivist Enlightenment" and began to share the same environment with religion. They even argue that modernity has given birth to many anti-secularist movements.[14] In brief, the idea which proposes that modernity and secularism are identical is no longer valid. One can argue today that the world has become modern, but one cannot argue that religion has retreated from the world.

---

13 William H. Seatos and Kevin J. Christiano, "Secularization Theory: The Adventure of a Concept", vol. 100-101, *Secularization on Trial: The Future of the Religion in the 21 st Century,* Ali Köse (ed.), Istanbul, Ufuk Books, 2002, pp. 95-121.

14 Peter L. Berger, "Secularism in Retreat" *National Interest,* Winter 1996/97, vol.4, pp.3-12; Peter Berger 'The Desecularization of the World: A Global Overview' in Peter L. Berger (ed.), *The Desecularization of the World, Resurgent Religion in World Politics,* Washington: Ethics and Public Policy Center, 1999, pp.1-18.

Construction of Dialogue and Tolerance*

The coexistence of the followers of the three divine religions and the coexistence of their place of worship is not a new phenomenon that we are witnessing. This glorious scene is what Islam envisaged and has been trying to establish in the historical process in Cairo, Damascus, Mardin, Kayseri and Istanbul for hundreds of years.[1]

Dialogue between religions and cultures and tolerance among different belief groups has caught our attention and gained importance as a value of increasing importance over recent years. This development will not only help to eliminate prejudices of the followers of different belief groups about one another and lessen the matters of conflict among them, it will also contribute to the solution of many basic problems which form the common issues of humanity and which are still awaiting a speedy solution, such as hunger, poverty, unemployment, environmental pollution, natural disasters, drug addictions, spiritual pollution and terror. Humanity should no longer tolerate the cultural conflicts that should have been left in the depths of history, but which have been intentionally carried over to the agenda of today. On the other side of the coin, humanity, which is trying to bring religion into a new field of understanding, has managed to have a better grasp, due to bitter

---

* This speech was delivered in Antalya on the occasion of the inauguration of "the Center of Tolerance Between Religions: The Garden of Religions" on December 8, 2004.
1 For a case study on Muslims and Turkey *see* Ekmeleddin İhsanoğlu, *A Culture of Peaceful Coexistence: Early Islamic and Ottoman Turkish Examples* , Istanbul: IRCICA, 2004.

ʾxperiences over the last two centuries, of the importance of calls to peace and salvation that are made in the name of religion.

Our religion, Islam, attached great importance to the establishment of positive relations between individuals and religions, and has called for eliminating discrimination in the world and eradicating the moral degeneration and injustice that threaten humanity. Dialogue between the adherents of two different religions does not necessarily mean that they approve of the other's stance, but rather that they are trying to understand one another and to set up a healthy communication based on knowledge, emotion and action. In this context, as dialogue makes it possible for there to be an atmosphere of tolerance, enabling the recognition and understanding of one another, as well as providing sound and unprejudiced information about the other, this forms an important step in the general call for peace and permanent happiness in Islam.

Democracy is a very important tool that allows the human experience to develop in this century in a culture of respect for religious differences and living together. From the perspective of the universality and permanency of peace, democracy presents very rich possibilities for us. The developing attitude of religiosity and the culture of tolerance that exist in Turkey will have an important role in this field. There is no doubt that the historical experience that we have inherited from the Ottomans has contributed a great deal, allowing for the current Republic of Turkey to constitute such an outstanding experince. This is why different religions and cultures have succeeded in coexisting together over the past centuries in peace and tolerance in Anatolia and the Balkans. If we really desire to prevent religions from being the reason and source of violence and tension between us and to establish a peaceful environment, we should benefit greatly from the historical experience that this land witnessed over many centuries.[2]

---

2 For historical analysis of peaceful coexistence in Anatolia *see* Kemal H. Karpat, "Millets

We all know that the messages of all divine religions, with Islam at the forefront, contain important elements that encourage individuals to live in peace and tranquility. The negative developments that arise from historical reasons or from the differences in religions today have not emerged from the essence of religions, but rather from the interpretations of their followers and from the attempt to thrust religions into the field of international strategies and interests. It is for this reason that, in order to establish world peace and human happiness, we should adhere to the essence of our religions, and try to understand each other well.

Dialogue and tolerance means acknowledging the existing differences between each other, without exaggeration or without creating problems and the desire to coexist and to feel compassion for others. The greatest obstacles standing in the way of tolerance and dialogue are the desire to eliminate all differences, the attempt to shape and mold others and the giving of approval to others only when they resemble us. The divine religions order us to feel affection not only for the Almighty Creator, but also for what He has created. Talking about affection and tolerance alone is not enough; this will only be significant if we are able to share these feelings and reflect them in our behavior, using them as valuable tools for cooperation with the aim of establishing common peace for all of humanity. We are of the opinion that the fundamental thing in relationships between individuals and societies is to love each other by acknowledging the differences and regarding these not as problems, but as a source of richness.

---

and Nationality: The Roots of the Incongruity of Nation and State in the Post-Ottoman Era", in *Christians and Jews in The Ottoman Empire, The Functioning of a Plural Society*, Vol.1, Benjamin Braude and Bernard Lewis (eds.), 1982, p. 141-142; P. Dumont, "Jewish Communities in Turkey during the last decades of the nineteenth century in the light of the Archives of the Alliance Israelite Universelle" in *Christians And Jews in the Ottoman Empire, The Functioning of A Plural Society* Vol.1, Benjamin Braude and Bernard Lewis (eds.), 1982, p. 221-222; Donald Quataert, *The Ottoman Empire 1700-1922*, 2000, p. 177.

Two Cases for the Co-Existence of Different Cultures and Religions: Turkey and India*

I. Setting the context: The world in crisis and conflict

Modern societies are facing a number of problems at both national and international levels. These problems are increasing day by day and becoming global threats. As a result of globalization and communication networks even a problem that emerges in the remotest corner of the world becomes a problem for the whole of humanity. There is no doubt that many people are trying to find solutions to problems that influence our relationships with individuals and the larger society with which we communicate.

These problems seem to have made an impact on many areas of our life. In this context, I believe that historical experiences can contribute to the prevention of the conflicts, tensions and frictions that we face today. I believe that we should benefit from historical experiences and practices when trying to solve such problems; these should be tackled on the basis of peace and tolerance, while an environment of co-existence is created where the concept of common good is the prevailing force.

We must carefully re-examine historical experiences that allow for the existence and representation of different languages, religions and cultures in a social reality that is devoid of conflicts. We need to draw lessons from exemplary experiences in order to estab-

* This paper was prepared by Professor Ali Bardakoğlu, the President of Religious Affairs, and read at the "Second Symposium of Turkish-Indian Relations in History" organized by the Indian Council of Historical Research in New Delhi between 9-13 February 2005.

lish an administrative culture for the future on the basis of peace and toleration. In this regard, two countries, namely Turkey and India, provide rich historical experiences and modern practices. Both countries have accepted religious and cultural differences as an asset; they do not consider diversity to be a threat and thus have not tried to eliminate any such differences by oppression. When we look at the historical experiences and current practices in these countries we can see that there has been a process of preserving differences and diversity. In both countries, a political culture and a social practice have developed in which different religions, denominations and identities have preserved their existence. With their historical experiences, Turkey and India provide the modern world with a culture of co-existence that allows different religious and cultural identities to preserve and develop their vitality without falling into conflict. I believe that the experiences of Turkey and India should be shared by people on a global scale in order to overcome deeply-rooted conflicts that inflict heavy burdens on us and which make the world more unbearable every day.

I mentioned earlier that we face many problems today. Broadly speaking, we can divide these problems into two categories. The first category includes problems that threaten the future of humanity. These are starvation, poverty, unemployment, moral decay, inequality, oppressive political regimes, legal and educational problems and the destruction of historical and cultural values. The second category includes problems that are closely connected to the first one. These are a lack of understanding, toleration and dialogue among people and crises related to intolerance towards differences and co-existence despite diversity.

These problems do not concern only one region, country or community, but rather the whole of humanity on a global scale. Politicians, intellectuals and scholars need to have a sound knowledge of successful and historical experiences and practices that can address and overcome such problems. I believe that Turkey and

India can contribute to the solution, or at least to the alleviation, of these problems with their rich historical heritage and modern experiences.

II. The search for conflict resolution

Humanity needs solid, just and participatory references, experiences, sources and enduring examples if it is to find sustainable and just solutions to overcome global problems; these problems include social chaos and injustice, poverty, terror and violence, crime, corruption, ignorance and a lack of faith. In this context, Turkey and India provide historically tried and tested references and experiences. A tolerant, moderate and flexible system and social practice that is open to communication and free participation lie at the basis of these experiences. The perception and understanding of a religion which has developed in the context of such references, discourses and practices is the most powerful ingredient allowing for the co-existence of different cultural and religious values.

Turkey and India are two countries that have a history of a co-existence of differences in an atmosphere of respect and tolerance. Turkey inherited a cultural legacy of respect and tolerance from the Ottoman Empire, which had a tradition of co-existence for many centuries. Modern Turkey not only inherited a culture and tradition, it also inherited Christian and Jewish communities. As we will see later in this paper, members of the various faith communities were protected by a special mechanism under the Ottomans, which gave these communities a special status and did not oppress them because of their religious beliefs. Principles of Islam which tolerate differences and diversity and the legacy of previous civilizations that existed in Anatolia and their social practices contributed to the emergence of such a culture in Ottoman lands. Modern Turkey pursues the culture of tolerance towards other religions; this has been inherited from the Ottomans. My paper will focus on Ottoman and modern Turkish experiences regarding the co-existence of different religious and cultural communities. However, I will briefly touch upon India to show similarities between the two countries. These similarities constitute a common ground for co-operation between Turkey and India to work together to provide solutions for conflicts around the world.

III. The tradition of co-existence in India

India has a rich historical experience in terms of co-existence and establishing dialogue with members of different faith communities. The relationship and dialogue between various religious traditions, which were sometimes problematic but often constructive, date back to 3000 BC in India. In the modern sense, inter-religious dialogue began in the 16th and 17th centuries. In this period, a positive atmosphere had developed towards different religions and faith traditions. Moreover a more tolerant and pluralist understanding emerged in comparison with the standards of that period. In other words, a social and cultural practice of co-existence was constructed in India, the effects of which are still felt today.[1] On the other hand, Muslims and Hindus in India, where more than 100 million Muslims live, worked with each other in solidarity in the face of common problems, as proven by the struggles against colonial powers. There is no doubt that one of the important elements that contributed to the experience of co-existence was the religious traditions of India. I believe that Hinduism, as the largest religion of the country, has also contributed to the emergence and development of a culture of respect for other religions and faith traditions.

However, ethnic and religious nationalism started and gathered momentum in the second half of the twentieth century in this region as well. From time to time, such trends triggered events that threatened the culture of toleration and the tradition of peaceful co-exis-

---

1 James Massey, "Inter-Religious Dialogue in India with Special Reference to Islam: Positions, Experiences and Reflections". *Journal of Religious Culture / Journal für Religionskultur*, No. 10, 1997.

tence. Religious concepts and discourses were sometimes used to legitimize political and populist projects.[2] It is noteworthy that the democratic and participatory political structure of India confined and limited the effects of the radical wings. Despite successful attempts to curb extremist groups, a historical mosque in Ayodhya was destroyed and almost two thousand Indian Muslims were killed during the clashes in Ahmedabad in 2002. These events caused great distress in the Muslim world. There is no doubt that these events motivated the Indian administration to introduce more sensitive political measures to protect the culture of toleration with which this country has been associated for many centuries. It is meaningful that certain measures have been taken in the democratic system to prevent harmful movements. These measures are aimed at stopping intolerant movements that use violence and weaken social cohesion.

The democratic and secular structure of India[3] also contributes to the preservation of the culture of the co-existence of differences. The secular nature of the country enables the state to maintain an equal distance with all religions and to take political decisions on the basis of democratic principles. There are numerous religions and faith traditions in India. Toleration towards and respect for the differences make up the basis of this social structure. Preservation of this tradition is extremely important for India and for other countries.

After briefly touching on the situation in India, I would like now to move onto the experience of the Ottoman Empire and modern Turkey regarding the co-existence of different religions and cultures.

---

2 For more information *see* S. K. Sahu, "Religion and Politics in India", in *Religion and Politics in Comparative Perspectives* T. G. Jelen and C. Wilcox (eds.), Cambridge: Cambridge University Press, 2002, pp. 243-265.

3 On the development of the secular state in India *see* R. Baird, "Secular State and the Indian Constitution" in *Religion in Modern India*, R. Baird (ed), Delhi: Manohar Publications (1981).

IV. Religious differences (plurality) and the culture of co-existence in the Ottoman Empire

In a way similar to Indian experience, Turkey has also had a long history and tradition of the co-existence of different religious groups and faith communities. Modern Turkey has inherited this legacy and reproduced it in modern times. It is worth mentioning the Ottoman policy and its intellectual roots. Such a historical analysis will provide us with insight and contribute to projects of co-existence in the future.

Muslims scholars who deal with the issue of the co-existence of Muslims and non-Muslims divide the citizens (inhabitants) of a country into two main categories, "Muslim" and "non-Muslim", from the perspective of legal status. Therefore, in the historical experience of Islam, a minority was not an ethnic group, but rather consisted of all non-Muslims, all of whom had a special legal status in the Muslim state.[4]

The Republic of Turkey inherited the Ottoman experience and developed it, as modern Turkey was established on the remnants of the empire.[5] Although some of the sources and discussions about the establishment of the modern Turkish state do not emphasise this heritage, we see that the achievements during the Ottoman era continue with a new perception in modern Turkey. We observe that different faith groups and religious communities have lived side by side in the Ottoman state. This is a very significant fact, because such a peaceful and tolerant social order was established in a period when democracy, pluralism and concepts such as freedom of religious beliefs and practices were not on the agenda.

A meaningful range of liberties was established for non-Muslim

---

4 M. A. Aydın, *İslam ve Osmanlı Hukuku Araştırmaları*, Istanbul, 1996, p. 229.

5 For more details on Turkey's inheritance from the past *see* M. Meeker, *A Nation of Empire the Ottoman Legacy of Turkish Modernity*, Berkeley: California University Press, 2002, pp. 3-85 and pp. 372-396.

religious traditions under the conditions of that period. If we judge by the conditions of today's democratic expansions, these egalitarian policies may not seem ideal. However, when we look at the problem from a historical perspective, we can see that non-Muslims were recognised and given liberties centuries ago in the Ottoman Empire. Different faith groups under the sovereignty of the Empire were not forced to change their religion and convert to Islam. Their existence and legitimacy were accepted by the political authority. Members of the Greek Orthodox Church, the Armenian Church and the Jewish community were each recognized as a *millet* (nation/community).[6] In the Ottoman Empire the society was governed on the basis of respect for different faiths. Therefore, there was no differentiation or discrimination based on racial or linguistic principles. The concept of *millet* denoted belonging to a religious community. It had administrative and cultural dimensions referring to those people who belonged to the same religion or the same denomination.[7] Non-Muslims living in Ottoman lands were recognized as members of a religion or a denomination. Under this system, religious communities were able to preserve their traditions and oral culture and to keep these alive. Such an atmosphere was a source of identity, security and pride for the members of the communities concerned.[8] Each non-Muslim community was regarded as an independent religious group or *millet*.

As the historical experience shows, theoretical approaches that determine relationships between the Muslim majority and non-Muslim minorities became concrete policies and practices under the administration of Muslim rulers. During this process, freedom of religion and consciousness for non-Muslims and the protection

---

6 On the legal status of non-Muslim faith groups *see* M. Macit Kenanoglu, *Osmanlı Devletinde Millet Sistemi ve Gayrimüslimlerin Hukuki Statüleri (1453-1856)*, (Millet System and the Legal Status of Non-Muslims in the Ottoman State), (Unpublished PhD Thesis), Marmara University, 2001.

7 İlber Ortaylı, *Osmanlı Barışı*, Istanbul, 2004, p .29-30.

8 Ortaylı, p. 29.

of their places of worship were guaranteed. Moreover, they were allowed to practice their religious laws amongst themselves. These minorities were also granted freedom to establish independent schools and to teach their religions.

Religious freedom was also extended to legal practices. Non-Muslims were allowed to institutionalize their own legal systems and to administer their courts within their community according to the principles of their faith. As a result of this policy, the sale and use of goods prohibited by Islam was allowed within a non-Muslim community if there was no such ban in their religious laws.[9] Muslim rulers were held responsible for the protection of the lives and goods that belonged to non-Muslims. On the other hand, there was no restriction against employing non-Muslims in public offices.[10] The autonomy and freedom available to minorities in the Ottoman Empire attracted large numbers of displaced Jewish communities, who were among the victims of persecution in Spain, Poland, Austria and Bohemia. While Jewish communities in Russia, Romania and most of the Balkan states suffered from persecution due to anti-Jewish laws, Jewish communities established in the Turkish territory enjoyed an atmosphere of tolerance and justice.[11] Moreover, Turkey sheltered many Jews who fled Nazi oppression in the modern period.

When judged according to the standards of liberty and freedom

---

9 Aydın, p. 233

10 For the policies and practices towards non-Muslims during the Ottoman era *see* Kemal H. Karpat, "Millets and Nationality: The Roots of the Incongruity of Nation and State in the Post-Ottoman Era", in *Christians and Jews in the Ottoman Empire, The Functioning of a Plural Society Vol.1*, B. Braude and B. Lewis (eds.), New York: Holmes-Meier Publishers, 1982, p. 141-142; (1982), T. Küçükcan, "State, Islam and Religious Liberty in Modern Turkey: Reconfiguration of Religion in the Public Sphere", *Brigham Young University Law Review*, 2003, No. 2, p. 480-485; Bilal Eryılmaz, *Osmanlı Devletinde Millet Sistemi*, Istanbul,1992, p. 15.

11 Paul Dumont, "Jewish Communities in Turkey During the Last Decades of the Nineteenth Century in the Light of the Archives of the Alliance Israélite Universelle" in *Christians and Jews in the Ottoman Empire*, Benjamin Braude & Bernard Lewis (eds.) 982, p. 221–22.

of the period concerned, we can easily argue that non-Muslims enjoyed a remarkable amount of freedom; so much so that it would have been unthinkable for many states in the same period. Non-Muslims enjoyed several important freedoms which were later to become fundamental rights in the late nineteenth and early twentieth centuries. Non-Muslims in the Ottoman Empire enjoyed the freedom to select their religious leaders, build their temples, practice their religious rituals, ceremonies and festivals, open their religious schools and provide a religious education in these establishments in their own languages. These were important achievements in providing liberty in a period when no one talked about basic human rights; these were guaranteed by the Ottomans. In this period, authority in matters of internal legal matters and educational issues within the community was generally granted to religious leaders who were freely elected by the community concerned. Moreover, these minority communities enjoyed certain financial privileges. For example, lands belonging to churches and synagogues were exempt from taxes. The *millet* system provided freedom, not only in the area of religion and worship, but also in areas of civil law and politics. All of these policies and practices indicate that the dominant perception of religion and culture in the Ottoman lands developed in such a way that a formula that enabled faith communities of different religions to live together with the "other" was established.

V. Culture of co-existence and its expression in modern Turkey

The perception of religion in Turkey, religiosity in Turkish society and Turkey's experience in relation to religious tolerance and moderation has a particular significance in the Muslim world. Turkey has a relatively better transparency and a more dynamic social life. Moreover, it has a secular state and a flexible political system. Due to these characteristics, religiosity in Turkey and the perception of Islam in this country have a special place and value for the Muslim world, as well as for the Western world. Turkey's experience and current status in these matters provide a forum for co-operation and compromise. Turkey is a good example of co-operation and compromise with its political and legal system that constitutionally protects members of various religious communities and regards them as citizens. The dominant and wide-spread perception of religion in Turkey provides room for the existence of liberty and freedom for non-Muslim minorities. Based on its long historical experience, one can freely argue that the culture of co-existence and the moderate perception of religion in Turkey are able to contribute to the establishment of a foundation for sustainable peace by saving religion from being a source of violence, tension and conflicts between societies.

Today, Turkey emerges as a tolerant country that is open to dialogue and which supports an original perception of Islam in the world. The dominant and wide-spread understanding of Islam in Turkey is neither a radical nor an exclusionary one. A moderate perception of religion in Turkish society has long and deep historical roots. There are many reasons for the development of such a religious understanding. First of all, there has been a tradition of co-existence in Anatolia for many centuries which promotes a peaceful life-style. Secondly, Islam does not suppress a variety of religious interpretations or differences in tradition. It promotes a religiosity that is informed by knowledge and based on self-confidence. Thirdly, Sufi thought in Islam has reinforced love for humanity. Moreover, the last two hundred years in Turkish history, a time period that includes many reforms and developments, such as the announcements of the *Tanzimat* and the *Meşrutiyet* and the establishment of the Republic, as well as parliamentarian democracy, have all contributed to the emergence of a pluralist intellectual approach to the concept and reality of co-existence with the "other".[12]

---

12 On state-religion relations in Turkey and its implications for society *see* T. Küçükcan, "State, Islam and Religious Liberty in Modern Turkey: Reconfiguration of Religion in the

Although the majority of its population is Muslim, Turkey does not have a monolithic characteristic in terms of its understanding of Islam. Interpretations of Islam may differ according to the various Islamic groups. Different and sometimes opposing views and interpretations of Islam can be expressed and discussed freely in Turkey.[13] Islam encourages political participation, civil initiatives, justice and equality. Islam never oppresses opinions in the name of God.[14] If Turkish society has a moderate perception of Islam, despite the existence of some problems, this is something that we owe to the establishment and development of a democratic culture in Turkey. Here we should point out that the Presidency of Religious Affairs has also contributed to the emergence and institutionalization of social compromise, pluralism, a moderate understanding of religion and a religious life that refrains from excess. The moderate perception of Islam in Turkey, to which the Presidency of Religious Affairs has made meaningful contributions, is also inspired by the reality of various trends and different views, in addition to the freedom of expression for all these opinions. Turkey is a country where Islam and democracy can co-exist and democratic culture leads to religious diversity.

In conclusion, the Ottoman and modern Turkish experiences can provide extremely important insights that will help to prevent conflict and friction in the field of religion, both in the Muslim world and in the West. In Turkish historical tradition all religions have co-

Public Sphere", *Brigham Young University Law Review*, Volume 2003, No: 2, 2003, pp. 475-506; F. Ahmad, 'Politics and Religion in Modern Turkey' *Middle Eastern Studies*, 27 (1), 1991, pp. 3-22; M. Heper, 'Islam, Polity and Society in Turkey: A Middle Eastern Perspective' *Middle East Journal*, Vol. 35, 1981, pp. 343-363; Ilter Turan 'Religion and Political in Turkey' in R. Tapper (ed.) *Islam in Modern Turkey*, London: I.B. Tauris, 1991, pp. 31-55.

13 For more information *see* Hakan Yavuz, *Islamic Political Identity in Turkey*, Oxford: Oxford University Press, 2003; Yasin Aktay (ed), *Modern Türkiye'de Siyasi Düşünce: İslamcılık*, Cilt. 6, Istanbul: İletişim, 2004.

14 *See* Ali Bardakoglu, "İslam ve Demokrasi Üzerine" (On Islam and Democracy), *İslamiyât*, Vol. 2, No: 2, 1999, pp. 77-84.

existed, for the most part in peace, and have developed their religiosity. The fertile religious tradition and rich heritage of the Ottomans have served as a basis of religious understanding and toleration that has been further developed under the democratic and secular structure of Turkey. Within this structure, the Presidency of Religious Affairs has an overall responsibility for the provision of religious liberty and its protection. The Presidency pursues a policy that protects religious and cultural diversity and regards such a variety as an asset for society. The Presidency fully supports the project of co-existence by preserving cultural and religious diversity.

Modern Turkey has tried to establish a balance between religion and secularity by constantly developing its democratic culture. Turkey differs from many other Muslim countries in that people of this tolerant country have a different understanding of Islam, because of its historical experiences and intellectual trends. As mentioned earlier, the moderate understanding of Islam, which is widely held in Turkish society, has historical, social and institutional roots peculiar to Turkey.

VI. Conclusion

Social, political and economic steps must be taken on local, national and international levels to find a solution for the problems and crises that threaten our future. However, these steps are not sufficient on their own for a sustainable solution. In addition to social, political and economic steps, humanity's cultural, religious and historical heritage should also be taken into account to find effective and sustainable solutions. In my view the cultural, religious and historical heritage that humanity has created to date can also make a meaningful contribution to our efforts to eliminate threatening conflicts. In this context, religions in particular have much to say that can guide people. Universal religions teach us that the protection of human life and dignity are a universal duty. They urge us to establish justice and stand against oppression and tyranny. India and Turkey constitute two examples for the reconstruction of the tradition and culture of co-existence, as both countries have historical experiences and modern-democratic political systems that can contribute to the solution of the problems we mentioned earlier.

To conclude, the Turkish and Indian experiences of centuries of toleration and co-existence in a cultural and religious diversity, despite occasional problems, are important models that can inspire many other nations and states in preventing conflicts around the globe. Historical and current practices show us that, although from time to time some minor problems occur, all religions have co-existed freely in peace, developing their own religiosity and institutions. This experience may serve humanity as a source of inspiration to add a spiritual dimension to the search for solutions to the current crises in the world.

Islam and Democracy in Turkey*

Dear guests,

It is an honour for me to be with you to share my thoughts on such important issues as Islam and democracy, the freedom of religion, and the co-existence of diverse faith communities in a secular nation state that has a dominantly Muslim population.

I would like to thank the organizers for creating this opportunity and hope that my remarks will shed some light on these issues and answer some of your questions.

Let me begin with some observations about the conditions of humanity today in order to set a context for my analysis. I am afraid that such an analysis will remain only abstract and unrealistic if we do not develop a good understanding of the social, cultural and political context of the challenges we face.

Although my observations may, at times, seem to be pessimistic, let me assure you that I have great expectations for the future because we, as humans, possess sufficient intellectual and spiritual resources to make this world better. We merely need to re-discover our spiritual strength and heritage and demonstrate the will to build a peaceful world.

Now let me turn to my observations. Modern societies are facing a number of problems, which are increasing day by day and becoming global threats, on both the national and international

---

* This paper was presented at a conference held by Saint Louis University, USA, on 11 April 2005.

level.[1] Even a small problem in the remotest corner of the world quickly becomes a serious issue for the whole of humanity as a result of globalization and modern communication networks.

Broadly speaking, these problems may be divided into two categories. The first one includes poverty, inequality and educational challenges that threaten the future of humanity. The second category, which is related to the first, includes the sad reality that we face on a daily basis: intolerance toward differences, the absence of dialogue and a lack of understanding. Such challenges create a major obstacle that stands in front of our goal of peaceful co-existence in a diverse world. These problems do not concern only one region, country or community, but rather the whole of humanity on a global scale; unfortunately they are not easily solved. Politicians, academics and scholars need to have a sound knowledge of successful experiences and practices to address and overcome such problems. If we do not develop a better understanding of each other, if we do not allow for the participation of different groups in public life and if we do not stop the abuse of religion for political justification, conflicts will no doubt increase in the future. I believe that these problems can only be solved through building a peaceful and tolerant social and political environment of co-existence where the concept of the common good is the prevailing force.

Let me emphasize the need to re-visit and carefully examine our historical experiences that acknowledge not only the existence but also the representation of different languages, religions and cultures in society. This is important, because as we know, history is of full of examples to the contrary. If nothing more, we need at least to draw lessons from such experiences in order to build a political culture for the future, based on peace and tolerance.

I would like to take the opportunity to talk about our experiences

---

1 *See* Peter Worsley (ed.), *Problems of Modern Society: A Sociological Perspective*, Harmondsworth: Penguin Education, 1973, Rene Guenon, *The Crisis of the Modern World*, London: Luzac and Company Ltd, 1975.

in Turkey; both our distant and recent history offer rich precedents for the development of the democratic culture in contemporary Turkey. Both in the past and in the present, Turkey has embraced religious and cultural differences as an asset. It has not viewed diversity as a threat and thus has not attempted to suppress diversity to mould it into a monolithic culture. If we look at historical experiences and current practices we will see that there has been a process of preserving differences and diversity. From a thriving Jewish community to various Christian communities, from Sunni Islam to other Islamic denominations, these religious traditions have shaped contemporary Turkish society. In this sense, Turkey has developed a system in which Islam, democracy and the secular state system go hand in hand.

As we all know, humanity needs proper references, experiences, sources and examples to find sustainable and just solutions to the global problems that plague our world, such as social chaos and injustice, poverty, terror and violence, corruption, ignorance, and, we must say, a lack of faith. To make this world, including the Middle East, a better place, and to overcome deeply-rooted conflicts in the region, which have inflicted a heavy burden on us on a daily basis, I believe we should take lessons from Turkey's experience with Islam, democracy and the secular state system. Turkey provides historically successful references and experiences that are marked by a tolerant and moderate cultural legacy, as well as a social practice that is open to free participation. The perception and understanding of Islam which has developed in the context of such references, discourses and practices is the most powerful element of the culture of co-existence in Turkey. In this context, I call upon Muslims and members of other faith groups to be aware of the fact that democratic culture and democratic values are not in conflict with Islam.[2] As many of you know, Turkey is a secular state with a

---

2 Ali Bardakoğlu, "İslam ve Demokrasi Üzerine" (On Islam and Democracy), *İslamiyât*, Vol. 11, No: 2, 1999, pp. 77-84.

dominantly Muslim population. However, it is also home to diverse cultural and religious communities, all of which go towards strengthening democracy. In order to show how democratic culture has been nurtured in Turkey, including the freedom of religion and expression, let me now give an account of the trajectory of Turkish history; what Turkey has achieved today has some historical roots that will be examined here.

Roots of democratic governance: Empire, Islam and other faith groups

Turkey is a secular state with a majority population that is Muslim. It has inherited a tradition of co-existence and tolerance, which is one of the key tenets of democracy, from the Ottoman Empire. Some of you will recall that the Ottoman Empire embraced diverse religious and cultural communities in a peaceful co-existence for many centuries. As we will shortly see, members of various faith communities were protected by a special mechanism under the Ottomans, which gave these communities a special status preventing any infringements of their basic or religious rights. First of all, the basic tenets of Islam recognizes differences and diversity. Also, the legacy of previous civilizations in Anatolia offered the Ottomans much in the way of tolerance and co-existence. The contributions of both sources explain the emergence of a culture of tolerance in Ottoman lands.

One might say that modern Turkey's commitment to a culture of tolerance is largely indebted to Ottoman practices as well as to modern values. The Republic of Turkey inherited this Ottoman practice and developed it further; modern Turkey was founded on the legacy of the Ottoman Empire.[3] Although the standard discourse about the establishment of modern Turkish state does not empha-

---

3 *See* Michael Meeker, *A Nation of Empire: The Ottoman Legacy of Turkish Modernity*, Berkeley: University of California Press, p. 3-85, 2002, pp. 372-396.

size this dimension, it should be noted that the achievements of the Ottoman era were continued with a new sensibility in modern Turkey. We can observe that different faith groups and religious communities lived side by side under the Ottomans. Their existence and welfare was legally and religiously sanctioned. It is very significant that such a peaceful and tolerant social order was established in a period when democracy, pluralism and concepts, such as the freedom of religious beliefs and practices, were not the norm in many other places.

The scope of liberties that was provided for non-Muslim religious traditions under the conditions of that period was certainly efficient and meaningful. If we judge by the conditions of today's democratic measures, this egalitarian policy may not seem to be the ideal. However, if we look at the problem from a historical perspective, we will notice that non-Muslims were recognized by law as communities of faith and given liberty to practice their traditions. They were not forced to abandon their religions and convert to Islam, nor were they compelled to settle their disputes in Islamic courts. Their existence was recognized by the political authority, so these communities had the option of choosing either authority to settle internal matters. Similarly, the Ottoman system recognized the differences that existed even within a faith community. Thus, it recognized the Greek Orthodox Church, the Armenian Church and the Jewish community as separate religious communities under the law.[4]

Since society was governed on the basis of legally recognized faith communities, linguistic and ethnic discrimination did not pose a serious threat. On the contrary, Ottoman policy fostered a sense of respect for different faiths within the Empire. Non-Muslims living in the Ottoman lands were recognised as members of a religion or

---

4 On the legal status of non-Muslim faith groups *see* M. Macit Kenanoğlu, *Osmanlı Devletinde Millet Sistemi ve Gayrimüslimlerin Hukuki Statüleri (1453-1856)*, (Millet System and The Legal Status of Non-Muslims in the Ottoman State), Unpublished PhD Thesis, Marmara University, 2001.

denomination. Under this system, religious communities were able to preserve and advance their traditions and oral culture. Such an atmosphere was a source of security and pride, and a marker of identity for members of the communities concerned.[5] Each non-Muslim community was regarded as an autonomous religious group. Freedom of religious practice and the protection of places of worship were guaranteed. Moreover, these faith communities were allowed to practice their religious canon laws amongst themselves. These minorities were also granted educational freedom to establish independent schools to teach their religions and traditions.

Religious freedom was also extended to legal practices. Non-Muslims were allowed to institutionalize their legal system and to administer their courts within their community according to the principles of their faith. As a result of this policy, the sale and use of goods which were prohibited by Islam was allowed within a non-Muslim community if there was no such ban in their religious laws.[6] Muslim rulers were held responsible for the protection of the lives and goods belonging to non-Muslims.[7] On the other hand, there was no restriction against the employment of non-Muslims in public offices.[8] The autonomy and freedom available to minorities under the Ottoman Empire attracted large numbers of displaced Jewish communities, among whom were the victims of persecution in Spain, Poland and Austria. While Jewish communities in Russia, Romania and most of the Balkan states suffered from persecution due to anti-Jewish laws, Jewish communities in Turkey enjoyed an

---

5 İlber Ortaylı, *Osmanlı Barışı*, Istanbul, 2004, p. 29-30.
6 M. A. Aydın, *İslam ve Osmanlı Hukuku Araştırmaları*, Istanbul, 1996, p. 233.
7 Bilal Eryılmaz, *Osmanlı Devletinde Millet Sistemi*, Istanbul, 1992 p. 15.
8 For more detailse *see* Kemal H. Karpat, "Millets and Nationality: The Roots of the Incongruity of Nation and State in the Post-Ottoman Era", *Christians and Jews in the Ottoman Empire: The Functioning of a Plural Society*, B. Braude and B. Lewis (eds.), New York: Holmes-Meier Publishers, Vol. I, 1982, p. 141-142; T. Küçükcan, "State, Islam and Religious Liberty in Modern Turkey: Reconfiguration of Religion in the Public Sphere", *Brigham Young University Law Review*, No. 2, 2003, pp. 475-506.

atmosphere of tolerance and justice.[9] That Turkey welcomed many Jews who fled the Nazi oppression in the 20th century is a little-known fact.

Therefore, judged from the point of view of the standards of liberty and freedom in the period concerned, we can easily argue that non-Muslims enjoyed a remarkable freedom that was unthinkable in many other states at the same period. Non-Muslims enjoyed several important privileges, which became recognized as fundamental rights only in the late nineteenth and early twentieth centuries. Non-Muslims in the Ottoman Empire enjoyed the freedom of selecting their religious leaders, building their places of worship, practicing their religious rituals, ceremonies and festivals, opening religious schools and providing a religious education in their own institutions and in their own languages. Legal authority in matters of internal legal and educational issues was also generally granted to religious leaders who were freely elected by the community concerned. Furthermore, these minority communities enjoyed certain financial privileges. For example, lands belonging to churches and synagogues were exempt from taxes. The system provided freedom not only in the area of religion and worship, but also in areas of civil law and politics. It is clear that these were important achievements in a period when few talked about such basic human rights. Such policies and practices helped the prevalence of a culture and public religiosity that appreciated co-existence with the other. This was the legacy that has been transmitted to the Turkish Republic of the 20th century.

Religion and democracy in modern Turkey

The perception of religion in Turkey, religiosity in Turkish soci-

---

9 Paul Dumont, "Jewish Communities in Turkey During the Last Decades of the Nineteenth Century in the Light of the Archives of the Alliance Israélite Universelle" in *Christians and Jews in the Ottoman Empire*, Benjamin Braude & Bernard Lewis (eds.), 1982, p. 221–222.

ety and Turkey's experience with religious tolerance and moderation has a particular significance in the Muslim world. Turkey has relatively better political transparency and a dynamic social life than most Muslim countries. It has a secular state and a democratic political system. Despite a few interventions, Turkish democracy has already achieved a remarkable standard, although it still has some way to go to achieve all that is necessary in this direction. For all of these reasons, the Turkish perception of Islam has a special place and value for Muslim countries, as well as for the Western world. Turkey's experience with these matters to date provides a forum for co-operation and compromise.

Turkey displays a good example of co-operation and compromise thanks to the political and legal system that protects the members of various religious communities and regards them as citizens. The dominant and widespread perception of religion in Turkey provides room for the existence of liberty and freedom for non-Muslim minorities. Based on Turkey's long historical experience, one can easily argue that the culture of co-existence and a moderate understanding of religion have the potential to contribute to the creation of a sustainable peace by removing religion from being a source of violence, tension and conflicts.

Today, Turkey emerges as a tolerant country that is open to dialogue. It promotes an original understanding of Islam that is neither radical nor exclusionary. As I have briefly mentioned, the moderate perception of religion in Turkish society has long and deep historical roots: First of all there is the tradition of co-existence in Anatolia for many centuries, which promoted peaceful life styles. Secondly, and perhaps more importantly, Islam acknowledges and recognizes diverse religious interpretations and differences in tradition. Islam promotes a religiosity enriched by knowledge and based on self-confidence. Thirdly, Sufi thought in Islam has reinforced love for humanity. Moreover, the experience of the last two hundred years in Turkish history, including modernization, legal, educational and constitutional reforms, as well as the establishment of the Republic and parliamentary democracy, have all contributed to the emergence of a pluralist intellectual view that embraces the concept and reality of co-existence with the religious or cultural "other".-

Although the majority of its population is Muslim, Turkey does not have a monolithic approach to understanding Islam. The interpretation of Islam differs according to various Islamic communities. Different and sometimes opposing views and interpretations of Islam can be expressed and discussed freely in Turkey.[10] This is a great opportunity for democratic maturity and for religious dialogue. This reality no doubt requires a secular state system, a separation of state and religion, and thereby a domain for the freedom of religion. If Turkish society has a moderate understanding of Islam, we owe this to the establishment and development of a democratic culture in Turkey. On the other hand, Islam does not condone the suppression of opinions in the name of God.[11] The basic tenets of Islam themselves encourage political participation, civil initiatives, justice and equality. These are also the principles of democratic thought. As democratic culture is not a property of a single culture and religion, there is no reason therefore to doubt that Islam and the culture of democracy can harmoniously work together.

I should point out that the Presidency of Religious Affairs has also contributed to the emergence and institutionalization of social compromise. It has encouraged a moderate understanding of religion, recognized diverse views and practices and helped to curb extremism. The moderate perception of Islam in Turkey, to which

---

10 For more information *see* Feroz Ahmad, *The Turkish Experiment in Democracy: 1950-1975*, Boulder: Westview Press, 1977; Hakan Yavuz, *Islamic Political Identity in Turkey*, Oxford: Oxford University Press, 2003; Yasin Aktay (ed.), *Modern Türkiye'de Siyasi Düşünce: İslamcılık*, Vol. 6, Istanbul: İletişim, 2004; Niyazi Öktem, *"Religion in Turkey"*, *Brigham Young University Law Review*, Volume 2, Number. 2: 2002, pp. 371-403.
11 *See* Ali Bardakoğlu, "İslam ve Demokrasi Üzerine" (On Islam and Democracy), *İslamiyât*, No. 2, 1999, pp. 77-84.

the Presidency of Religious Affairs has made meaningful contributions, is also inspired by the reality of various trends and different views. I must also acknowledge the impact of the freedom of expression, which guarantees the articulation of diverse opinions in the public sphere. I hope that my brief observations have shown that the harmony of Islam and democracy is sustainable in Turkey and that a democratic culture helps promote a healthy religious diversity. Here, I would like to emphasize once more that the Ottoman and modern Turkish experiences can provide significant insights into preventing conflicts and friction in the fields of religion and state, both in the Muslim world and in the West. How is the Turkish experience a source of inspiration? The answer to this question lies in the fact that the Turkish experience is an original one in the Muslim world. Now let me explain why it is original and therefore why it requires special attention.

What is the originality of the Turkish Experience? What makes Turkey different?

Modern Turkey tries hard to strike a balance between religion and secularism by constantly developing its democratic culture. Partly for historical reasons and partly because of a conscious will, religiosity in Turkey has evolved and is evolving in a direction of more tolerance and accommodation. In this it differs from many other Muslim countries.

For over 80 years modern democratic culture has existed and is continually improving in Turkey. During this time, Turkey has been able to forge and sustain legal, cultural and social institutions that assure the continuation of the democratic culture and religious tolerance. Now Turkey shines as an exemplary experince among other Muslim countries, promoting a democratic culture that fosters tolerance, participation, civil society and moderation.

No one would deny that the Muslim world faces grave challenges as far as democracy and relations between the state and religion are concerned. At times, and in certain countries, Islam is used for political justifications and to prevent democratic change. I must plainly express here that the religion of Islam does not stand in the way of democracy in the Muslim world. On the contrary, Islam is being used against its basic tenets and as a code name to express ideas against democracy. It seems to me that the main obstacles standing in the way of democracy are regional conditions and conflicts, anachronistic traditions as well as the nature of international relations which narrowly focuses on those national and international interests that are not necessarily supportive of democratization. I must also note with regret that there seems to be reluctance among some politicians in the West to embrace the establishment of democracy in the Muslim world.

Islam in Turkey is not monolithic. Intellectuals, scholars and leaders of religious groups can freely express their views of Islam. There is no restriction on critical thinking in Islam, and Turkey enjoys a diversity of views. In contrast, many other Muslim countries lack such a free platform. In some Muslim countries there is strict support for only one school of thought and there is a state policy to suppress opposition. Where there is no freedom to express diverse interpretations, uniformity and rigid understanding of Islam prevail and no room is left for moderation and tolerance. If this rigid and monolithic interpretation of religion is enforced on people, it will eventually lead to fanaticism. Turkey has an opportunity in that there is room for all views, and the state does not take a stand on any particular interpretation.

It is not only a religious duty, but also our duty as human beings to take advantage of the universal message and basic teachings of Islam in order to help prevent violations of basic human rights in society and to inform others of the same, striving to prevent all examples of such negative behavior in society. That is why I believe that a proper democracy can only be put into practice by guaranteeing the rights of women.

Many reforms have been launched in Turkey with abiding faith in the vital importance of women in society that give Turkish women equal rights and opportunities. Being aware of the problems women are facing today, the Presidency of Religious Affairs has also taken an active role in finding solutions, developing and adopting lasting policies to remedy the challenges faced by women today.

As I stated earlier, Muslims should be conscious of the fact that a democratic culture and democratic values do not contradict Islam.[12] I believe that a democratic culture and democratic values certainly contribute to the emergence of such moderation, which is the innate nature of Islam. Some of you will recall the verse in the Holy Qur'an that reminds the believers that God created them to be a moderate nation so that they will act as witnesses to the whole of humanity. Let me stress also that I am of the opinion that Muslim scholars should no longer support authoritarian regimes and oppressive political cultures. As scholars we must not provide religious justification for such leaders and governments. We must promote the idea of a civil society, and encourage the participation and accountability of the political elite. We must foster the view that Islam is not opposed to the existence of different religions or religious groups in a Muslim society. And we must be defenders of human rights, such as the freedom of religion, thought and expression, because Islam calls us to be just, to protect the oppressed, to love our fellow humans and to be merciful to the needy and the weak, as well as to those under our protection. Islam provides a myriad of spiritual as well as intellectual resources for the creation and maintenance of a democratic culture.

---

12 Ali Bardakoglu, "İslam Kültüründe Din ve Vicdan Özgürlüğü" (Freedeom of Religion and Conscience in Islamic Culture), in *Osmanlı Devletinde Din ve Vicdan Özgürlüğü* (Freedeom of Religion and Conscience in the Ottoman Empire), Istanbul: Isav Publications, 2000, pp. 41-57.

Conclusion

At the beginning of my talk I highlighted the conditions of humanity and stated that we face numerous challenges today. Social, political and economic steps must be taken on local, national and international levels to find solutions to the problems and crises that threaten our future. However, these steps are not sufficient on their own for a sustainable solution. In addition to social, political and economic steps, the cultural, religious and historical heritage of humanity should also be taken into account in order to find effective and sustainable solutions.

In my view the cultural, religious and historical heritage that humanity has created to date can also make a meaningful contribution to our efforts to eliminate conflicts. In this context, religions in particular have much to say that can guide people. Islam, like other universal religions, teaches us that the protection of human life and dignity is a duty for all. Islam urges us to establish justice and to stand against oppression and tyranny. I firmly believe that Turkey constitutes a good example for the culture of democracy and co-existence.

Enriched by a long historical legacy, the Turkish experience with religion and state, which we call Islam and Democracy, is a significant one that may inspire other nations on the road to democracy and prevent conflicts around the globe. It may also serve humanity as a source of inspiration to add a spiritual dimension to the search for solutions to the current crises in the world. I would like to stress again here that the Turkish experience demonstrates that Islam and Islamic culture cannot be reduced to a monolithic tradition, even within one country. With its own particular characteristics the Turkish experience with Islam and democracy should be seen as an opportunity to establish a bridge between the West and the Muslim world.

Thank you for your attention.

The State and Religion in Modern Turkey*

Ladies and gentlemen,

I am honored to be with you today. It is a privilege for me to share my thoughts on the state and religion in Modern Turkey. I would like to thank the organizers for creating this opportunity for me. I hope that this talk will shed some light on the issue of the state and religion in modern Turkey and answer some of your questions.

As the title of my talk suggests, I will focus on the relation between the state and religion, including modernization and secularization in Turkey. You may ask why we should talk about Turkey, or what is the significance of the Turkish experience? In my view, Turkey as a secular nation state with a rich historical legacy and dominantly Muslim population needs to be carefully examined. Such an examination will yield many clues regarding how Islam and democracy, religion and modernization can exist in secular nation state. A study of modern Turkey will also provide some answers to the questions that many Muslim nations are facing today.

Now let me justify why Turkey stands out as an important case study in understanding state-religion relations, the establishment of democracy and the emergence of a moderate perception of Islam. The following questions, which I will try to answer in my talk, indicate the importance of the Turkish experience. What makes Turkey different from other Muslim countries? What are the sources of the

* This paper was presented at a conference held by the University of Chicago, The Center for Middle Eastern Studies, USA, on *13 April 2005*

moderate perception and understanding of Islam in Turkey? Can Islam and democracy coexist? How far can democracy establish freedom for religious diversity?

In order to answer these questions properly we need to place Turkey in its social, political and cultural context. Otherwise, if we are unable to perceive the continuity and change which Turkey has undergone, we will not be able to find the correct answers.

When considered in this context we may understand the Turkish experience better by keeping the following classifications in mind: (i) the Ottoman experience, (ii) the process of modernization and secularization, (iii) the tradition of intra and inter-religious dialogue that also made democracy and secularization stronger, (iv) the function of the Presidency of Religious Affairs regarding modernity and dialogue.

Now let me share my views with you about what makes Turkey special and different from many other countries. First of all, Turkey occupies a unique place among the modern nation states. Turkey lies at the crossroads of eastern and western strategic, political and economic interests, not only from a geopolitical, but also from cultural and religious points of view. On the other hand, Turkey possesses a cultural and religious legacy from many civilizations. It has inherited a great legacy from the past and has re-interpreted it in line with modernity. When we examine the Turkish experience we can see that modernization, democratization and secularization all started before the establishment of modern Turkey. Therefore, it is important to examine the roots of these developments when analyzing the Turkish experience.

Legacy of reform: sources of modernization, democratization and secularization

In the later periods of the Ottoman state and society, modern western ideas were already present. Ottoman statesmen and intellectuals laid the grounds of modernization and westernization. These efforts were widely accepted and expanded on by the early republican elite circles in the formative period of modern Turkey. The Turkish Republic inherited and adopted some of the ideas and practices of the old regime.[1] Therefore, it is necessary to look at how modern ideas entered and started to shape Turkish political culture during the Ottoman Empire.[2]

Starting from the late 16th and early 17th centuries, the Ottoman Empire entered a period of military and economic decline. This led to the emergence of new ideas on the necessity of reforms in political, economic and military fields, as well as in the area of education.[3] Broadly speaking, modernization, westernization and secularization in the Ottoman Empire can be viewed in several periods, caused by significant events. Early modernization efforts and western influences can be traced back to the impact of the French Revolution; by the late 18th and early 19th centuries, the Ottoman State had started to lose control over the periphery of the empire.[4]

The Ottoman legal system was based on the Islamic legal system. As an important part of the modernization and westernization process, secular laws were introduced, although the mainframe of Islamic law was protected and codified. The secularization of the

1 Ergun Özbudun, "The Continuing Ottoman Legacy and the State Tradition in the Middle East", in *Imperial Legacy: The Ottoman Imprint on the Balkans and the Middle East*, (ed) L. Carl Brown, 1996, p. 133.

2 Feroz Ahmad, *The Making of Modern Turkey*, London: Routledge and Kegan Paul, 1993, p.15; for a detailed examination of the imperial legacy on the Turkish Republic *see* Michael Meeker, *A Nation of Empire: the Ottoman Legacy of Turkish Modernity*, Berkeley: University of California Press, 2002, pp. 3-85.

3 Niyazi Berkes, *The Development of Secularism in Modern Turkey*, London: Hurst and Company, 1998, pp. 24-27.

4 For authoritative discussions on this issue *see* Stanford J. Shaw and Ezel Kural Shaw, *History of the Ottoman Empire and modern Turkey: reform, revolution and republic, the rise of modern Turkey, 1808-1975*, Cambridge: Cambridge University, 1977; Roderic H. Davison, *Reform in the Ottoman Empire : 1856-1876*, Princeton: Princeton University, 1963; Selçuk Akşin Somel, *The Modernization of Public Education in the Ottoman Empire: 1839-1908 Islamization, autocracy and discipline*, Leiden: E.J. Brill, 2001.

law started before the establishment of the secular Turkish Republic. Thus the position of the Sheikh-ul-Islam was removed from the cabinet and the Sharia courts were brought under the control of a secular ministry of justice. Traditional institutions of learning (*madrasas*) were also brought under the control of the Ministry of Education and a new program was introduced for them.

Religion and secularization in Turkey

Political, social and religious developments in modern Turkey were marked by the ideals of modernism and secularism.[5] The separation of religion and politics was seen as an essential step to opening the doors to western values. Therefore, secularism was adopted as one of the foundation stones and central tenets of modernization, as it was thought to be indispensable to its accomplishment.[6]

There were some significant secularization reforms in the symbolic sphere. The alphabet was changed from Arabic to Latin.[7] Western style of clothing was introduced.[8] The Gregorian calendar was adopted. Western music was taught in schools. The weekly holiday was changed from Friday to Sunday.[9]

The first step in institutional secularization was to abolish the Caliphate, to start a transformation from an *ummah* to a national entity. With the abolition of the Caliphate, the principles of politi-

---

5 Kemal Karpat, *Modern Turkey*, in *The Cambridge History of Islam*, P. M. Holt, et al (eds.), 1970, vol I, p. 528; Yael Navaro-Yashin, *Faces of the State: Secularism and Public life in Turkey*, Princeton: Princeton University Press, 2002.

6 Walter F. Weiker, *The Modernization of Turkey*, New York: Holmes Meier, 1981, p. 105; S. M. Akural, "Kemalist Views on Social Change", in *Atatürk and the Modernization of Turkey*, (ed.) Jacob M. Landau, 1984, p. 126.

7 B. Lewis, *The Emergence of Modern Turkey*, London: Oxford University Press, 1968, p. 398; G. L. Lewis, "Ataturk's language Reform as an Aspect of Modernization in the Republic of Turkey", in *Atatürk and the Modernization of Turkey*, (ed.) Jacob M. Landau, 1984, p. 195; Karpat, op cit, p. 535.

8 Andrew Davison, *Secularism and Revivalism in Turkey*, New Haven: Yale University Press, 1998, p. 150.

9 Akural, *op cit*, p. 45.

cal legitimacy were changed so as to exclude Islam as a source of legitimacy and political loyalty to the state. Despite the abolition of the Caliphate, however, the Constitution of 1924 still preserved Islam as the state religion.[10] But later in that year, the office of the Şeyhülislam and the Ministry of Religious Affairs and Pious Foundations were abolished.[11] However, in the same year the office of the current Presidency of Religious Affairs was established.

Functional secularization was carried out by the secularization of the court system and by the introduction of the Law for the Unification of Instruction (*Tevhid-i Tedrisat*), under which all educational establishments came under the control of the state.[12] Legal secularization was accomplished by the adoption of a new civil code[13] based on a Swiss code.

Despite the secularization effort of the public sphere and promotion of secular values, Islam remained as one of the major identity references. And it still continues to be an effective social reality that shapes the fabric of Turkish society.

The religious profile of modern Turkish society and the role of the Presidency of Religious Affairs (the Diyanet)

Approximately 99 percent of the population in Turkey is Muslim. However, Islam is not a monolithic religion. Although the majority of the Muslim population belong to the Sunni interpretation of Islam, the current perception and practice of Islam varies from mystical to folk Islam and from conservative to a more moderate one. In addition to the country's Sunni Muslims there are also Alawis groups as part of the larger Muslim community. In fact, the

---

10 Karpat, *op cit*, p. 533-4.
11 Stanford J. Shaw and Ezel K. Shaw, *History of the Ottoman Empire and Modern Turkey: Reform, Revolution and Republic*, Cambridge: Cambridge University Press, 1977, vol 2, p. 384
12 M. Winter, "The Modernization of Education in Modern Turkey", in *Atatürk and the Modernization of Turkey*, Jacob M. Landau(ed.), 1984, p. 186, Berkes, op. cit., p. 4
13 Shaw and Shaw, op. cit., vol 2, p. 385.

Alawi perception of religion cannot be treated as something outside of Islam. There is a great diversity of interpretation in the history of Islam. Alawis, like the Sunni majority, do not possess a monolithic structure either. They have a diversity of interpretations and dozens of competing associations which reflect the varieties of Islam in Turkish society.[14]

As pointed out earlier, the Republican elite abolished a number of institutions as part of the modernization program. The traditional offices responsible for delivering religious services were also closed down. However, the modern Turkish state claimed the responsibility for the organization and administration of religious affairs. Therefore, the Diyanet was established as a public institution. The Diyanet was made responsible for the administration of religious affairs in the areas of Islamic faith, practices and moral principles. The organization of mosques and the task of informing people about Islam also became primary responsibilities of the Diyanet. When we look at the aims and the organization of the Diyanet, we can see that it did not merely emerge as a bureaucratic institution, but rather as part of a project to establish moral religiosity.

The establishment of the Diyanet can also be seen as a response to the problem of sustaining public stability in the area of religious affairs and as a way to meet the public demand for satisfactory religious services. Here, I would like to underline the fact that the absence of a clergy in Islam does not mean that religious affairs are administered casually or that religious services are provided in a disorganized manner in Muslim societies.

The organizational structure and functions of the Diyanet

1- The Diyanet is a public institution: It is, structurally, part of

---

14 See İlyas Üzüm, *Günümüz Aleviliği*, (Contemporary Alawism), Istanbul: TDV İsam publications, 1997; İlyas Üzüm, *Kültürel Kaynaklarına Göre Alevilik* , Istanbul: Horasan Yayınları, 2002; David Shankland, *The Alevis in Turkey*, London: RoutledgeCurzon, 2003.

the state mechanism and the bureaucratic system. The Diyanet's place in the state organization and whether this contradicts the secular nature of the state has been an ongoing controversial issue among legal experts and scholars in Turkey. This issue is related to how one understands secularism. The position of the Diyanet within the state organization is not in contradiction with secularism, according to the following principles that are upheld in Turkey: (a) Religion should not be a dominant or effective agent in state affairs. (b) The provision of unrestricted freedom for the religious beliefs of individuals and religious liberties are under constitutional protection. (c) The prevention of the misuse and exploitation of religion is essential for the protection of public interest. (d) The state has the authority to ensure the provision of religious rights and freedoms as the protector of public order and rights.

The Diyanet is not a Sunni organization, since it has a public character representing all Muslims with different religious backgrounds and practices. It does not follow a policy towards spreading the Sunni interpretation of Islam either. It embraces a policy to provide Muslims with a true knowledge of Islam, but it allows people to find their own way.

2- The Diyanet is an independent institution: The Diyanet enjoys freedom in scholarly activities, in intellectual discussions of Islamic issues and in the production of religious knowledge. Here, I would like to emphasize that the Diyanet conducts its affairs freely without any restriction when providing religious services.

It plans and executes its policies and practices based on scholarly findings and experience. Utmost care is given in making the best choices and finding the most original solutions among all available interpretations, without external pressure. At this point, I would like to draw your attention to our understanding of secularism in Turkey.

Secularism in Turkey does not mean the exclusion of religion from our lives. It means the separation of the affairs of religion and state. This does not mean the intervention of the state in the interpretation of religion, because such an intervention would contradict the very essence of secularism.

Secularism in Turkey provides freedom for individuals and public institutions in the interpretation of religion and in the production and transmission of religious knowledge. Therefore, the Diyanet exercises scholarly and intellectual freedom in its religious interpretations.

3- The Diyanet is a civil institution: The Diyanet emerged as a response to the religious needs of Muslim believers. Turkey has a predominantly Muslim population and the people need to learn about their religion freely in the light of authentic scholarship. The Diyanet was established to meet such needs in society; it, therefore, has a democratic and civil basis. In that sense, it does not have a policy of imposing a particular model of religiosity on people. It does not support an essentialist idea of Islam.

The Diyanet takes religious demands and traditional forms into account when delivering its services. However, if there is a departure from the shared and sustained perception, then authentic knowledge is promoted; the Diyanet tries to educate people about their religious beliefs and practices in the light of sound knowledge and scholarship.

These three (public, independent and civil) aspects of the Diyanet explain its current structure and function. They also indicate that the Diyanet faces numerous challenges as an institution.

Today, Turkey emerge sas a country that supports a moderate, tolerant and inclusive perception of Islam. The widespread perception of Islam in Turkey is not radical, fundamental or exclusivist. One of the reasons for such a moderate understanding of Islam in Turkish society is the fact that democratic culture has existed in Turkey for a long time. Since its establishment, Turkey has improved its democracy and now it acts as a good example among other Muslim countries. What we see in Turkey is that democratic culture promotes tolerance, participation, a civil society and moderation. It is clear that other Muslim countries and societies also need democracy today more than at any other period in history.

Conclusion

If we have a moderate perception of Islam in Turkey today, it is thanks to the establishment of democratic culture, which has played a great role in this achievement. I suppose democracy in return owes the moderate perception of Islam its ability to gain ground in Turkey. I would like to point out that the moderate perception of Islam in Turkey is also rooted in the fact that different trends, ideas and views of Islam can be expressed freely. As I mentioned earlier, the majority of the Turkish population is Muslim. But Islam does not have a monolithic nature in Turkey. The interpretation of Islam may differ from group to group. There is room for all views and interpretations.

As I stated at the beginning of my talk, Turkey offers an excellent example of a case study for those who are trying to find answers to the following questions: Can Islam and democracy co-exist? How far can religion and secularism be reconciled? To what extent can religious liberty be extended in a secular state? As the answers to these questions will show, the Turkish experience deserves a closer examination.

Religion Promotes Peace and
Condemns Violence*

The role of religion and its potential capacity to contribute to conflict resolution, peace building and the promotion of peaceful co-existence,[1] regardless of race, religion and language, requires an assessment of the global picture. Neither the influence of religion nor its employment by many actors can be understood without understanding the social, political and economic context. Therefore, if there is to be a fruitful discussion on religion and its relations with current events the context should be set first, as the context has important bearings on how and why religion is involved in recent debates on the subject. We need to avoid sociological blindness and take religion into account as an important factor in our analysis.[2]

Let me share some of my initial observations on the state of modern societies. Modernity opened new avenues for mankind but could not sole all the problems.[3] Modern societies are facing a num-

---

* This is the text of the speech delivered at the "Conference on Democracy and Global Security" organized by the Turkish National Police in Istanbul on June 9-11, 2005.
1 Douglas Johnston (ed), *Religion, the Missing Dimension of Statecraft*, New York: Oxford University Press, 1995; Ralph H. Salmi, Cesar Adib Majul, George K. Tanham, *Islam and Conflict Resolution Theories and Practices*, Lanham: University Press of America, Inc., 1998.
2 *See* Meredith B. Mc Guire, *Religion: the Social Context*, California: Wadsworth Publishing Co., 1992; Phillip E. Hammond and N. J. Demerath, *Religion in Social Context: Tradition and Transition*, New York: Random House, 1969.
3 For critical evaluation of modernity *see* Alain Touraine, *Critique of Modernity;* trs. David Macey, Oxford: Basil Blackwell LTD., 1995, Ted V. McAllister, *Revolt Against Modernity*, Kansas: University Press of Kansas, 1995; Leszek Kolakowski, *Modernity on Endless Trial*, Chicago: The University of Chicago Press, 1990; Charles Taylor, *The Malaise of Modernity*, Ontario: House of Anansi Press Limited, 1991.

ber of problems at national and international levels. These problems are increasing day by day and becoming global threats. Even a problem that emerges in the remotest corner of the world is becoming a problem for the whole of humanity as a result of globalization and improved communication networks. There is no doubt that many people are trying to find solutions to these problems that are influencing our relations with individuals and the larger society with which we communicate. These problems seem to have an impact on many areas of our life.

Broadly speaking, we can divide these problems into two categories. The first category includes problems that threaten the future of humanity. These are starvation, poverty, unemployment, moral decay, inequality, oppressive political regimes, legal and educational problems and the destruction of historical and cultural values. The second category includes problems that are closely connected to the first one. These are a lack of understanding, tolerance and dialogue among people and crises related to intolerance towards differences and co-existence despite diversity. These problems do not concern only one region, country or community, but the whole of humanity on a global scale.

Violence and terror, which have been on the rise in recent years, concern all of us. Religious symbols, discourse and rhetoric are used not only to justify these evil acts, but also used to recruit believers.[4] The social, economic and political problems mentioned above provide a fertile ground for such practices. Poor, oppressed and marginalized people become easy prey for recruits to terror groups and are willing to follow their instructions. As we have witnessed in recent years, religion has been hijacked into a cycle of violence, despite the fact that all universal religions condemn violence and promote peace.

---

4 Harvey Cox, *The Seduction of the Spirit: the use and misuse of people's religion*, New York : Touchstone Book, 1973.

As far as universal religions are concerned, the main messages revolve around peace, co-existence, the dignity of human beings, social justice and the moral community. In the establishment of these institutions and practices there is no room for violence and terror. In this context, let me remind you how Islam approaches the matter of taking a human life. One of the widely known principles of Islam is expressed as follows in the Qur'an "...whoever kills a soul is regarded as if he has killed the whole of mankind and whoever saves a life is regarded as if he has saved the lives of all mankind..." (al-Maida: 5:32) This verse clearly indicates the sanctity of human life. Another Qur'anic verse also emphasizes the importance of humanity as follows: "And surely, we honored the children of Abraham". (al-Isra: 17:70) There are many other examples, both in sacred messages and historical experiences, that religion is source of peace. It has a powerful spiritual capital for social peace, integration, conflict resolution and development. As religious leaders, it is our duty to underline the spiritual capital and capacity of religion in order to prevent the abuse of religion by terrorists. However, religious leaders and faith communities cannot solve this problem on their own no matter how hard they work. As I have explained earlier we need to tackle the deeper social, economic and political problems that provide a fertile ground for the recruitment of terror organizations.

Social, political and economic steps must be taken on local, national and international levels for the solution of problems and crises that threaten our future.[5] Even these steps are not sufficient on their own for a sustainable solution. In addition to social, political and economic steps, human cultural, religious and historical heritage should also be taken into account to find effective and sustainable solutions. In my view the cultural, religious and historical heritage that we have created as humanity so far can also make a

---

5 Barrington Moore, *Reflections on the Causes of Human Misery and Upon Certain Proposals to Eliminate Them*, Boston: Beacon Press, 1973.

meaningful contribution to our efforts to eliminate threatening conflicts such as terror. In this context, religions in particular have much to say that can guide people. It is therefore our duty to share our views with policy makers and with the public to show that religions can serve humanity as a source of inspiration and add a spiritual dimension to the search for solutions to the current crises in the world.

Faith, Solidarity and Co-operation*

In the name of Allah, the Most Beneficent and the Most Merciful

Honorable spiritual leaders, distinguished guests,

Ladies and Gentlemen,

I would like to begin by thanking God Almighty, who created us, blessed us as human beings, and gave us the ability to live together in peace. Praise be upon all the prophets, including Adam, Abraham, Moses, Jesus, and our Prophet Muhammad, who brought the message of God as a blessing to all humanity.

First, I pray for those who died or suffered because of the earthquake in Pakistan and Kashmir and in other natural disasters that have taken place recently. May God's mercy be with those who lost their lives and may God save all human beings from such natural disasters and help us to reach a lasting peace among all civilizations.

Dear Guests,

The problems that modern societies face today are many; some are caused by natural disasters, like earthquakes and floods; others are manmade ones, like wars and conflicts; some have physical affects, and others have moral and spiritual implications. There are many national and international problems we have to overcome. If

---

* This is the text of the speech delivered at the Second Conference on Peace and Tolerance, Istanbul, Turkey, November 7-9, 2005.

these problems are not tackled effectively, they will soon become global threats for us all.

It seems that poverty, inequality and lack of education threaten the future of humanity. There are also such problems as intolerance of differences, absence of dialogue and a lack of understanding that we are constantly facing. Such challenges stand in the way of a peaceful co-existence in a diverse world and threaten not just one region, one religion or one civilization, but the whole of humanity. Therefore, we are all responsible for dealing with these problems, not with words, but with actions.

Dear Guests,

I believe that one of the most effective steps to solve such problems is to establish ways for a strong dialogue between religions as well as cultures. Such a dialogue will not only help to wipe out the prejudices of the followers of different faiths, but will also contribute to solve the above-mentioned problems. I believe that a lack of sincere dialogue causes the discourse of the clash of civilizations to gain ground. I am, however, optimistic for the future because we are able to make the world better and we have enough intellectual and spiritual resources to confront these problems. What we need is merely to re-discover our spiritual strength, and to show the will to build a peaceful world. And this can only be achieved when we fully realize that action speaks louder than words.

I see no obstacle to Islam establishing such a sincere dialogue, because Islam maintains that sincerity is the core of all human acts. Islam has agreed on inter-religious dialogue since its very first day. Islam, from the beginning, has encouraged and supported a healthy relationship among all individuals, societies and cultures. Yet, one should bear in mind that dialogue in this sense does not mean that the faith of others has been accepted, but rather that there is understanding and communication between the faiths. I know very well that the approach of other religions to dialogue is no different. And

I firmly believe that it is not the religion itself that causes negative outcomes, but rather the various interpretations of it. Such an attitude gives way to the abuse of religion in the arena of international politics, which leads to distrust and suspicion between parties. And when suspicion is prevalent, any initiative by great powers to solve global problems is perceived as having a hidden agenda other than humanitarian one.

Dear Friends,

I would like to stress that we must stand against any kind of radicalism, extremism or violence that is carried out in the name of religion no matter, what reasons or sources they have. We sadly witness today that religious symbols and rhetoric are used throughout the world to justify these evil acts.

We, as religious leaders, should stand firm in declaring that violence can have no justification from religion. It should be our duty to underline that religion cannot be abused by the actors of terrorism. Yet, we should also be aware that religious leaders and religious communities cannot solve this problem on their own, because the matter does not emerge directly from religion itself. It has social, economical and political aspects, which provide a fertile ground for violence.

It is therefore our duty to warn and enlighten our political leaders that the multi-cultural and multi-religious structure of societies should be maintained. We must consider the multi-religious and multi-cultural structure of our societies as valuable resources in our struggle against radicalism, extremism and violence. I believe that it is equally harmful to force communities to have a monolithic structure. That is why a lasting peace in the Balkans, Caucasus, Central Asia, and anywhere else can only be achieved by preserving the variety of religious and the cultural traditions.

It is clearly an error to think that another society can be our friend only when we are able to influence it. This is as uncivilized as it is unholy. The Qur'an is very clear in this sense. God says: "We have created you of a male and a female, and made you tribes and families that you may know each other." (Hujurat 49: 13).

There are ways in which our efforts for dialogue and cooperation can lead to unintended consequences. We should, therefore, observe some principles in this respect. First of all, dialogue should not prevent us from expressing the truth in our religions. Here again, we need to make a distinction between expressing the truth and exploiting cultural differences for 'religious' aims; furthermore, peaceful coexistence with religious and cultural diversities should be preserved and encouraged; and finally any kind of initiative to solve the global problems such as poverty, inequality, and lack of education must remain loyal to its stated goals and should not be manipulated for political purposes.

Distinguished guests,

The Presidency of Religious Affairs has taken active roles in developing and adopting projects for cooperation among different religions and cultures. And we will surely continue to do our best to find solutions to the challenges which may emerge in the future.

I thank you all and pray to God to give us strength in our spiritual journey for a more peaceful future.

Global Ethics and Islam*

Ladies and gentlemen,

It is a great pleasure for me to be with you today. I hope this meeting on global ethics will contribute to our common efforts to live in a more peaceful and ethical world. I also hope that it will contribute to the development of a mutual understanding of the views and values of one another.

I believe that modern societies today are facing a number of problems on national and international levels. These problems are increasing day by day and posing global threats. A problem that emerges in the remotest corner of the world soon becomes a problem for the whole of humanity due to the forces of globalization that are felt so strongly.

Broadly speaking, we can divide the problems we are facing today into two categories. The first includes such problems as poverty, inequality, violence and terror, racial and religious discrimination and a lack of education.

The second includes problems closely connected to the first category. These can be cited as a lack of dialogue and tolerance towards differences, as well as a negligence of moral and religious values. These problems do not concern only one region, one country or one community, but the whole of humanity on a global scale. Politicians, intellectuals and scholars, indeed everyone needs to have a common approach in order to address and overcome such problems.

---

* This speech was delivered at the closing reception of "Global Ethics Conference" organized by the University of Chicago, 13-14 April 2005.

If we do not develop a better understanding of one another, if we do not stop the abuse of religion for the justification of political interests, and if we do not give proper attention to religious and moral values, conflicts will certainly increase in the future.

I believe that these problems can be solved by establishing a positive interaction between religion, morality and life.

I can assure you that the Presidency of Religious Affairs in Turkey is aware of this issue. We are giving our full attention to this matter and making every effort to achieve our aims. We are very proud that the services we provide for the public always emphasize the importance of moral values and individual religiosity.

I believe that our perception of Islam in Turkey has a good foundation for achieving this goal. Today, Turkey emerges as a country that cultivates a moderate, tolerant and inclusive perception of Islam. The widespread perception of Islam in Turkey is not radical, fundamental or exclusive; democratic values, intra and inter-religious dialogue and co-existence of different views have a rich history in Turkish society.

Yes, Turkey is a secular nation state with a majority Muslim population. Secularism means the separation of the affairs of religion and state. It does not mean the exclusion of religious and moral values from our lives. Therefore, morality, in addition to beliefs and rituals, occupies a central place in the fabric of Turkish religiosity.

We are very much aware that religion is not the only source of morality, but that every religious person must be a moral person.

I hope again that this meeting will contribute to our common efforts to establish a peaceful world.

I will leave you with a saying of the Prophet Muhammad, peace be upon him: "I have been sent only to perfect morality."

Appendix

Address to the Ambassadors of OIC Member Countries*

Your Excellencies, Distinguished Guests,

It is a great honour to welcome you all to this iftar dinner. I am extremely pleased to see that all of you have been able to come.

I should express my sincere thanks to each of you for sharing this friendly atmosphere on the occasion of Ramadan, which is a time when the Muslim world prays, and a time for humanity.

First, I would like to remember the victims of the recent earthquake in Pakistan and Kashmir. I pray for God's mercy on those who lost their lives. May God help and protect all human beings, not only from natural disasters, but also from man-made tragedies as well.

Although natural disasters can never be prevented, we may, nevertheless, lessen the pain and suffering that they cause on the victims. For this purpose, a donation campaign has been started at the Presidency to collect money in the mosques throughout Turkey for the victims of this earthquake as a first step; our support will continue and our hearts will be with them.

Dear Guests,

As you all know, today's common values, such as human rights,

---

* This speech was made at the iftar diner given by the State Minister Professor Mehmet Aydın and the President of Religious Affairs Professor Ali Bardakoglu on October 18, 2005.

freedom, democracy, tolerance, care for the environment, respect for the rights of others and so on, are the very values that we, as Muslims, have cherished throughout our history. Islamic civilization has played a major role in the development of these values. Moreover, peace, which is the desire of all nations today, is an essential element of Islam. However, we, as Muslims, have not always represented our values in an effective way.

As we all know, the Muslim world faces many problems and challenges at present. The source of these problems, however, is by no means, Islam. Rather they originate from various conditions, such as regional conflicts, economic inequality, social imbalance and political ideologies that prevail in Muslim countries.

The Muslim world, however, is not alone in confronting these problems. The developed countries have many social and spiritual crises as well. We may not be able to find a common space for cooperation if we blame one side and vindicate the other. Responsibility falls upon us as all human beings.

The Presidency, with its leading capacity and resources, has expended great effort to teach a sound knowledge of Islam and to provide better religious services by establishing a balance between the demands and traditions of Muslims and the common values of the contemporary world.

Interview

By *FATMA DEMIRELLI*
Ankara - Turkish Daily News
May 10, 2004

Professor Ali Bardakoğlu is the President of Religious Affairs who has perhaps received the largest share of media attention of all who have held that position. A few months after his appointment in May 2003, the Turkish media started to call him a "reformist" leader, and this image was strengthened even further when he decided, in a radical move, to replace his black gown, traditional for all Presidents of Religious Affairs, with an ivory-colored gown.

Sitting in his very modern office, a serious-looking Bardakoğlu says he is unhappy with his "reformist" tag and emphasizes that he has never aimed at reforming religion, something that Islam does not allow. According to him, the talk of reform closely associated with his tenure stems from confusion between religion and the thoughts people subjectively hold about the religion; when he speaks against a tradition, which people wrongfully see as religion itself, he is immediately seen to be promoting reform in religion.

"For instance, saying that religion consists not only of performing prayers is not a call for reform," he said in an interview with the Turkish Daily News, emphasizing that the ethical dimension of religiosity should be restored and that people should be told that an understanding of religion devoid of ethics can never be a proper one.

Shifting from Islam to the way Islam is perceived in today's world, Bardakoğlu says that there was an understandable reaction against the West in certain parts of the Muslim world; he urges the West to abandon an oversimplified approach that links violence to Islam's nature and to look from a social scientist's perspective to determine the reason for this reaction. That social approach, however, does not mean that he is supportive of the U.S.-floated Greater Middle East Initiative, as he is cautious that incorrect methods may be employed and he makes clear that Presidency has never been part of such a political project. He also dismissed prospects for Turkey being a model in the Islamic world, saying that Turkey is only able to share its unique experience with those countries that are willing to do so.

Concerning Islam and terror, Bardakoğlu categorically dismisses any involvement of Islam in violence and terror incidents that have been perpetrated by extremists. "Islam has existed for 14 centuries. Why are such things happening now?" he asks.

He defends his Presidency in the face of criticism that they have contravened secularism and says that the Presidency of Religious Affairs (the Diyanet) has freely determined what to tell people, independent of state influence. Bardakoğlu states that the management of religious services by private parties rather than by the centralized Diyanet would be potentially dangerous and lead to clashes between different groups under the current circumstances.

The full text of the interview with Professor Bardakoğlu is as follows:

TDN: Since becoming the new head of the Presidency of Religious Affairs, your name has been associated with "reform" and you have often been referred to in the media as a "reformist" leader. Can we talk first about this reform issue? Why have you come to be known as a reformist and what is your vision as the President of Religious Affairs?

BARDAKOĞLU: Actually, I have not used this word and do not

think that it is proper to use it. I have said on different platforms, several times, that there can be no reform in religion. Religions have been sent to humanity, and human beings are to benefit from them as much as they can. What we need to review here is not the religion itself, but our religiosity. I have never talked of modernization in religion. This is out of the question, and what is written in the Qur'an is clear. This was our message. Islam does not allow reform and it is not open to reform.

Wishes for reform

TDN: Then why do you think that such things were said after you became the President of Religious Affairs?

BARDAKOĞLU: I can tell you about two kinds of expectations. First, some people expect an explanation of religion that is in accordance with their way of life, and thus they would like to see religion made to suit their needs, rather than changing themselves to suit the religion. According to the understanding of such people, religion should be reformed and a new interpretation of religion should be introduced that accommodates their way of life. But this is not possible. The nature of religion does not allow this. Secondly, there are people who consider their traditional beliefs and the interpretations of religion that have been handed down to them as the original religion. In their belief, changing such interpretations means changing the religion. However, what is being reviewed here is not the religion, but the historical religious experience, and any additions that have been made to the religion throughout its historical course. Religion and religious experiences are different things. Religion means a message that is valid forever, while religious experiences refer to different ways in which this message is understood and put into practice in different societies in different periods of history. Therefore, religions never change, but religious experiences do change. At times, we come up with a critical attitude and say there could be different opinions. This can be seen as a reform or modernization attempt in religion by those people who see traditional interpretations as being the same as religion, and therefore this can be criticized. So, the talk of "reform in religion" stems from expectations on the part of some people for an explanation and interpretation of religion that suits and accommodates their way of life, while at the same time there is criticism on the part of those who disapprove of any different views on religious practices and experiences.

TDN: Was it your critical attitude towards religious experiences and the way religion is practiced that has led to you being labeled with the tag of a "reformist"?

BARDAKOĞLU: I don't think I have made any serious criticisms in this field. Today, the question of how we should understand religiosity is very important. An understanding of religion that is more modern, that is better at promoting peaceful coexistence and which puts a greater emphasis on compatibility in human behavior with ethical norms — this is what we want to see. Religious ethics are crucial, and we have to rebuild them today. We have to make it clear that religiosity necessarily requires being moral. Religious but immoral — this is out of the question. When we have said these things, they have been perceived as a call for reform.

Misperceptions are not religion

TDN: Then, what you have said has been received as something that is new.

BARDAKOĞLU: Indeed, these are not new things. These are what Islamic scholars have agreed on, and this is what the original message of Islam is. For instance, saying that "religion does not consist solely of performing prayers" is not religious reform. These are not novel things, but people tend to see their way of life as being the essence of religion. You face resistance if you suggest anything different. For instance, we have said that women should be able to perform prayers in more comfortable parts of mosques. This did not create a huge problem, but rather rumors were sparked as to whether the Presidency of Religious Affairs wanted women and men to perform their prayers side by side in the mosques. Women should be able to enjoy the time that they spend in mosques; this is not reform, this is what Islam says in its original message. Similarly, we spoke out against "honor killings" because religion sees family honor as an important thing, but does not legitimize "family councils" convening and deciding to kill women. Killing women in the name of honor and discrimination against women is against our religion. No religion could ever support such a tradition. To live an honorable life is something that all people have to do, and women are not more responsible than men in this regard. But saying this does not mean that we are making a call for reform in religion. Our call is for a religion the same for all, not exclusive to this or that sect or group. People can build their different interpretations on the common ground that we have explained and on the basic principles that the entire Muslim world agrees upon. The rest is an issue of personal freedom. And while doing this, we must stick to the original sources of religion, rely on methods to produce knowledge, take into account the contemporary world and the sociological dimension of religion. This automatically enables us to fight against the exploitation of religion, superstitious beliefs and fanaticism, while keeping in mind that criticism and accusations are not the right way to convince people to accept truths about religion. What we should do is to promote good examples instead of launching campaigns against the misperceptions we see.

TDN: This all sounds very logical and easy to accept. Yet it seems there are some incongruities with what people witness in reality. The Muslim world has become the center of attention for the rest of the world in the era of post-Sept. 11th, and what they see there looks a bit different.

BARDAKOĞLU: It is sad to say that Sept. 11th has proven us to be right. I wish that tragedy had never happened and that we had never been proven right, but it happened. There is a serious reaction against the West in certain parts of the Islamic geography. But to say that this reaction stems from religion would be wrong. Islam has been on the earth for 14 centuries; why is this reaction happening now? The right question to ask would be how, from a social scientific perspective, we should analyze this anti-Western reaction, its roots and why some religious arguments have been integrated into that reaction. Very serious attention should be paid to this question. The Western world, on the other hand, seems to be choosing the easy way out and an over-simplified answer, saying that the root of the problem is Islam and that Islam always produces terrorism. This is wrong; no religion produces terrorism. But this oversimplified argument both serves the missionary understanding and has become a means to justify the West's international policies. The truth, however, is that the shared values of a society always tend to be used as a tool for justifying movements that emerge within that society. There is ground in certain parts of the Islamic world that is suitable for the emergence of violence and terror. But this ground is not religion; it stems from frustrations that have nothing to do with religion, and the reaction that emerges in return is justified by religion. What we need is a more socio-scientific approach here. We have to analyze the economic situation and income level in the countries concerned. We have to analyze the impact made by authoritarian regimes and their foreign support.

The incorrect methods of the Greater Middle East Plan

TDN: It seems the U.S. administration is aware that those items mentioned above are already under consideration as part of the Greater Middle East Initiative. Do you think this is what the Islamic world needs?

BARDAKOĞLU: What matters here is what is going to be used

as a means and what method is to be taken to reach the goals. Using the wrong methods for good and just ends cannot be right. With good words and bad deeds, you will end up in a situation where people will question if you really meant your pleasant words or whether they are being used simply to achieve hidden, bad objectives; or, even if you mean what you say, how ethical is it for the end to justify the means? That is, how ethical would it be to violate human rights in order to bring about human rights or to launch a war and shed blood to introduce democracy? Whether it would be possible to transfer a political and social model from one part of the world to another is another question. Exporting mentalities is against the basic logic of social sciences. Certain things must come from our own dynamics.

We at the Presidency of Religious Affairs have never considered becoming part of international projects. Such projects are exclusively related to states and governments. What we do is to explain Turkey's experience, the understanding of religion in Turkey and our advantages and weaknesses in this understanding. This is not politics, but an explanation of religion. One condition of living together is to be empathetic, to have insight into the way other people think and see that there is a reason for a person thinking in a particular way. It would be a step in the right direction if the West were to make better analyses of the reaction in the Islamic world as well. Keeping all this in mind, I have often spoken in the West of how Islam is a religion of moderation, a religion of tolerance, that it backs coexistence and could never produce terror or violence. This is what we can see in our Turkish experience. Our understanding of religion is flexible enough to allow the coexistence of different cultures. This has been the case since Ottoman times, and this is why we do not have a monolithic religious structure in Turkey. On the contrary, we have a richness of variety. Secularism and democracy provide a certain guarantee to make sure that this richness will continue. The separation of religion from politics and freedom of religion are principles that have been well established in Turkey. In Turkey, secularism is no longer debated. Republicanism and Kemalism are no longer issues of controversy here.

Moderate Islam

TDN: There has been a new debate about whether Turkey presents a case of "moderate Islam". Do you think that Turkey is such a country?

BARDAKOĞLU: No, I do not approve of this expression. It gives the impression that there is an alternative to Islam proper and that we are choosing that alternative, renouncing the original Islam. The concept of "moderate Islam" makes one think that we are making efforts to redesign Islam in a way that would suit certain people. But this is not true. We cannot explain Islam to people by making it softer than it actually is or by making it more moderate. We can only explain what Islam is. We do not use the term "moderate Islam"; this somehow implies an Islam that has been made moderate and redesigned according to prevailing circumstances. But our religion does have moderation. It has tolerance and coexistence as well. There is no extremism or radicalism, there is no forcing others to do the things we do or to believe in the things we believe. As for extremism, it does not come from religion; it is a political stance, a political attitude. In Turkey and elsewhere, Islam has always been moderate. There could be places where extremism is rampant, and we have to carefully analyze the reasons behind it. And for that we need Islam to be well explained to people.

TDN: You must have explained all this during your meetings in the United States earlier this year. What do you think? Do you feel the Western world has understood your message, or do you see a kind of stereotyped understanding of Islam still in place?

BARDAKOĞLU: Of course, it is out of the question that what they think and what we think should be identical. It would be naive for me to expect people who have been living in a different culture and who have been provided with serious misinformation about a different religion throughout their life to have opinions similar to mine. What I see is that Islam has not been properly explained to the Western world. It has been described in a way that suits expectations which have been in place for a long time. They speak of an Islam that reflects their own tendencies, their own expectations and what they want to see. I have suggested that they try to see the living religious experience in Turkey and religion as a sociological phenomenon, not the religion that they want to see. Islam as written in original sources has no problems, no contradictions. Unless provoked, religion never leads to trouble among people. Living Islam is what Westerners must see.

'Model' debate: Disrespect for other countries

TDN: Do you believe Turkey can be a model for the Islamic world, as the U.S. administration appears to be suggesting? Where does Turkey stand vis-à-vis the Islamic world?

BARDAKOĞLU: To say that Turkey is a model for others would be disrespectful to others. This is nothing more than an idealization of ourselves. Either way, it is wrong. To talk of being a model for other countries goes against the courtesy of international relations as well. Similarly, a social scientist cannot talk of one country being a model for another country. Countries can only share their experiences with each other. I do believe that Turkey is a good model in the way that it understands and interprets Islam and that it is a step ahead of other countries in this respect. But this is a subjective assessment; another person could easily perceive their own country as a good model. What Turkey should do is to promote itself and present its case to the outside world. It should open up to the world and make effective use of what it has. This is what I have tried to explain in the United States. If somebody else follows our course, that would be a positive development, yet if they don't, that does not mean we are somehow in the wrong. We have a very rich accumulation of religious knowledge, a legacy from the Ottoman Empire, and our doors are wide open to anybody, from the West or the Islamic world, that wants to share it.

TDN: You say the concepts of secularism and Islam are well established in Turkey, but certain arguments from the EU and domestic critics apparently are at odds with that view. Based on some of these arguments, can I ask you to comment on the criticism that a secular state should not have an institution like your Religious Affairs Presidency and that its existence goes against the principle of state secularism?

BARDAKOĞLU: I don't believe that the existence of the Presidency of Religious Affairs contradicts the principle of secularism. The Presidency of Religious Affairs is a project of the Turkish Republic and it is indeed a very sound project. It is not the state that decides on the religion that is explained to the public; we do it freely, on our own. Any suggestion from the state would be against the principle of secularism, since in a secular order the state cannot define and describe the religion. In Turkey, the Presidency of Religious Affairs was created as a public institution, and it performs a very positive and useful service by properly organizing and coordinating religious services for the public. In this sense, it is a state institution, but in terms of determining what information we should rely on while providing these services, we are completely independent and rely completely on our own methods, knowledge and initiative. While choosing what to tell the public, we take into account the religiosity of the people as well as the way in which they perceive religion. This is what makes us democratic and civilian. The Presidency of Religious Affairs has never been an institution that is at odds with secularism. This is particularly true when it is kept in mind that secularism does not mean that a state does nothing as far as religion is concerned. On the contrary, secularism means that politics operates independently from religion, on its own rational basis. It means that it is the statesmen, not the clergy, who govern the state. Being independent from religion does not mean ignoring religion; religion is a major phenomenon of society.

The private management of religious services may be harmful

TDN: What do you think the advantages of having a Religious Affairs Presidency are? In one of your earlier speeches, you said that leaving religious affairs in the hands of private congregations, as occurs in many European countries, would be unacceptable. Are you saying that having a Religious Affairs Presidency is an alternative to that?

BARDAKOĞLU: Only when religious beliefs and religious education are better established and the risk of the abuse of religion for personal interests decreases can we talk about such matters. Personally, I don't think the management of religious affairs should be left in the control of communities or congregations yet. It might cause serious problems and might create clashes in the future. When I say congregations should not control religious affairs, I am not arguing for the state and its institutions having a say in every detail involved. And arguing against private congregations having control of the management of religious services does not mean that civilian societies and traditional opinions will be ignored, either. The religious sensitivities of society should be respected. That's why we are not providing a single version of religious services to people. At the Presidency of Religious Affairs we do not force any particular model on the people. We take the people's religious beliefs, opinions and sensitivities into account. This doesn't mean that we condone such beliefs or opinions. It is for this reason that we tell people that they shouldn't light candles or tie pieces of cloth to tombs. We try to inform the people and tell them what the appropriate religious behavior is, and then we leave them to make their own judgment. There are important religious choices. For example, in Turkey we call on people not to drink alcohol and ask them to fast during Ramadan. We try to explain the religion of Islam, which is supposed to be the unifying force of the people. Congregations and organizations will formulate their religious choices based on this unifying force. The Presidency of Religious Affairs has to provide a very balanced religious service.

TDN: Should religious services provided by the Presidency of Religious Affairs cover only Muslims, or should non-Muslims be included?

BARDAKOĞLU: If there is a consensus among communities, we could address non-Muslims as well. The Presidency could become the leading religious institution in Turkey. However, the Lausanne Treaty has provisions that would be contravened by such a situation. That's why I don't think non-Muslims would accept such an arrangement. The Lausanne Treaty provides minorities with a different status. This status does not fall under the authority of the Presidency. I believe that non-Muslims are satisfied with the current arrangement. Non-Muslims in Turkey have broad freedoms, and I don't believe they would be willing to abrogate them. However, I don't think that a single institution that manages all the affairs for all religions would be a bad move.

Alawite representation in the Diyanet

TDN: How much Alawite representation is there within the institution?

BARDAKOĞLU: Alawis are Muslims. They are just one of the groups within Islam. The Presidency has an understanding that covers all groups. The basis of the Presidency's teaching covers all beliefs. Everyone can express themselves differently based on this common stance.

TDN: Do you think the current representation is sufficient?

BARDAKOĞLU: It definitely needs to be developed. The Presidency has to develop an understanding that also includes the Alawis. It would be wrong to say the Presidency of Religious Affairs teaches only Sunni practices. We teach Islam. Our teachings are based on truth and scientific knowledge.

TDN: Have you had any dialogue with the Alawis?

BARDAKOĞLU: The current dialogue is weak because most of them say there should be no Presidency at all. Others say the Presidency is just an institution and that they should also establish an institution that covers their interests. They want to see themselves within a different competitive environment. This is also a mistaken opinion, but everybody sees themselves as Muslim and accepts the Presidency as their institution. We have no problems with the people. Organizations and representatives seem to have a problem, and behind this are some conflicts of power among these organizations. I believe the Presidency should have a standing that includes the Alawis. The perception that the Presidency has been open to Sunnis and closed to Alawis is also wrong. When we employ people, we don't ask what their beliefs are. Citizenship is the only important thing. A person's religious beliefs are their own business. There is no justification for establishing an Alawite bureau. There are no bureaus for other people.

Facts about wearing the headscarf

TDN: Last but not least, what is the Presidency's stance in debates concerning a ban on wearing headscarves in state institutions and schools?

BARDAKOĞLU: We never were party to the headscarf debates because the debates are mainly concerned with the political or legal nature of the issue. We make statements about the religious nature of the issue only. We have said: "The extreme and private beliefs of people are not important. What is really important is the 14-century-long Islamic experience. Muslim men and women have seen the headscarf as a religious requirement until now." There was no political angle in the past. Muslim women used to cover themselves due to their religious beliefs. When examining a religion, you have to take into account experiences, the living religion and sociological considerations. Saying: "I don't think headscarves are a religious requirement" does not solve the problem either. While it might not be the case, a majority of the population views it differently. Questioning the perception of the people will not resolve the issue. There are no serious religious discussions in Islam. And it is not up to us to say what we think about the matter being handled in state law. That's up to the politicians. We answer questions related to the religious aspects of the issues. We try to inform the people. It is apparent that the Islamic world believes that wearing the headscarf is a religious requirement. We cannot change this fact.

PRESS RELEASE
(World Women's Day- March 8, 2004)

Human rights, and more specifically the rights of women, which make up a large part of human rights, is not a matter that has newly appeared on the agenda. The fact that as a human being one is entitled to certain fundamental rights is one of the basic values that make up the message encapsulated in Islam. In Islam, the right of humans, who are all seen as honorable creations worthy of respect, to live among others enjoying all the same basic rights is seen to be immutable, entrusted to us by God.

It is a not only a religious duty, but also our duty as human beings, to take advantage of the universal message and basic teachings of Islam in order to help prevent violations of basic human rights in society and to inform others of the same, striving to prevent all examples of such negative behavior in our society.

The so-called "moral" or "honor" killing is only one of the problems faced by the women in our country. There are many more problems faced by women, be they in Turkey or in Western Europe. These problems do not arise from a religious source; they are caused by social, cultural, economic reasons, in addition to their being historical or geographical factors at play. A large factor that plays a role in the "honor" killings is the patriarchal attitude that brings the rights and property of men to the fore. This perception, which does not place a true human value on women, sees them, from the time they are born, as being inferior to men and as being a different being altogether. The Qur'an, as well as acquainting us with He who created men and women as separate but equal individuals, also openly condemns such a perception (Nahl 16: 58-59; Zukhruf 43: 17-18; Takwir 81: 8-9)

The fact that fourteen centuries after the Qur'an was revealed to us women still face discrimination, a matter that was censured by Almighty God, is saddening and thought provoking. Can we say that as parents we follow the example of Prophet Muhammad? He was an extremely interested, tender and merciful father to his daughters. He never tolerated any one to beat, forcefully marry or denigrate women or young girls. He gave the glad tidings that fathers who educate their daughters gain Paradise.

Despite all the warnings found in the Qur'an and the examples set by Prophet Muhammad, the education and development of girls and women at the start of the 21st century imposes on us all a myriad of responsibilities. Perhaps the most distressing aspects of this problem that needs to be focused on here is the negative concepts created by a section of society where a patriarchal attitude rules, concepts such as the "honor" killings of wives and daughters, domestic violence, and educational and sexual discrimination.

Although the concept of "good name", a concept in which is included ideas such as "chastity" or "honor", actually has a much wider scope, taking in a person's thoughts, intentions and all their actions, it has become limited to the physicality of a woman and set in a much narrower frame. To see this concept as only referring to women feeds another misconception that has been created by the mentality and traditions of society.

Almighty God has not just given us life and death; He has also bestowed rights on human life. The rights of humans are more important and take precedence over all other rights. Individuals, independent of official or legal bodies, do not have the authority to judge or punish. If a crime has been committed, a person only has the right to take legal recourse in order to make a complaint or to seek restitution. No family's mores can be seen as being above the law of the land. In no way can such crimes be justified with religion; they cannot be legalized. People who commit such murders are seen to be guilty both in the eyes of society and according to Islam as taught to us by God.

The "moral" or "honor" killing is one of the three most common types of violence that is practiced against women. This is why we have to face up to and struggle against the violence that exists around us now. But we must realize that this is a long, hard struggle. The state must cooperate with institutions and women's groups to delineate the fundamentals, dimensions and solutions to these problems, and the struggle against violence should become part of government policy. Everyone should participate in this, from educators to sociologists, from civil organizations to the media. To develop motifs that condemn the violence carried out in the name of honor, tradition and local culture is of the utmost importance.

At the Presidency of Religious Affairs we must be aware of the problems that are faced by women and take on an active role in the solution, developing and adopting lasting policies. To put these decisions into practice we need to get together with the relevant societies and women's groups. It is essential that we eliminate the concept of our religion as something that approves of violence against women; we must bring the correct understanding back into the light. We need to strive to live together in peace, to respect and love one another as human beings, teaching the lessons given to us by Islam in a lasting and structured manner.

We pray that World Women's Day, 8 March, brings everyone, women and men, happiness and peace, that it makes us more actively aware of human rights and sexual discrimination and that it may act as a new starting point.

PRESS RELEASE
(Incidents of violence – November 11, 2004)

We observe with deep sorrow the conflict and unrest that has directly affected world peace for years in the Middle East, Balkans and Caucasus and which has become an unavoidable human disaster in our neighbor Iraq. The taking of innocent lives, families being ripped apart, homeless and desperate children, places of worship being destroyed, a war which has become brutality, the reciprocation of violence with violence, the continuation of violence until its utmost limits, reaching even women, children, those who provide humanitarian aid and all of those who live in Iraq are all causing great distress to the rest of humanity and causing us to look with pessimism on the future. There is no justification for shameful antagonism that is directed towards the basic merits of humanity and its rights and freedoms.

Despite the terrible experiences that humanity has suffered over the last century, violence, terror, and wars have not come to an end. Abusing places of worship, which under normal circumstances should be representatives of peace and calm, destroying the common cultural heritage of humanity in this irresponsible way, killing children and innocent people without mercy, are not only shameful for the whole of humanity but are also crimes against humanity that should never be repeated.

The objective of Islam, sent to humanity as a heavenly message and form of guidance, is to realize order instead of disorder and enmity, to establish peace and justice in place of hostility and oppression. The Qur'an invites every believer to peace and urges the followers of the Divine religions to harmony and reconciliation. (Al-i-Imran, 64)

Nations that share the same world have to behave with understanding and impartiality towards each other. All prophets invited people to live in peace and brotherhood and urged them to respect basic rights. But these Divine principles have been violated, not only during the historical process, but also at the present time due to political and economic motives. It is for this reason that peace is non-existent in many regions today.

The most recent incidents which have been the means of planting the seeds of hatred and resentment between societies and supporters of different religions and cultures, a situation that is expected to continue for centuries with violence and brutality continuously escalating, will remain as a terrible stain on the history of humanity and will not be easily removed from our minds. This unfortunate situation will certainly create great difficulties for Muslim, Christian and Jewish religious officials who have to struggle desperately to establish and sustain world peace.

In this context, we invite all religious leaders to be initiators of peace, and appeal to politicians to listen to them carefully. The defenders of noble merits, like basic rights and freedoms, who are coexisting together in peace, mutual respect and affection, living with dialogue and tolerance, should waste no time in transmitting these values from the theoretical to the practical sphere. Those who are in power should in particular adopt an attitude that will help prevent this dreadful violence; humanity and history demand urgent cooperation so that these wounds can be bound without delay. We invite everybody to common sense, and to behave consciously and responsibly against all the incidents that might threaten the future of humanity.

INDEX

Tanzimat, 82.

Tevhid-i Tedrisat, 105.

Terror,

-abuse of religion, 19, 113, 117.

-association of Islam with terror, 45, 47.

-condemnation by religion, 111, 113.

-overcome religious violence, 19.

-rising in recent years, 112.

-sources of, 47, 112.

Ummah, 104.

UN Declaration on Intolerance and Discrimination Based on Religion or Belief, 41.

Universal Declaration of Human Rights, 41, 42, 50.

Violence,

-abuse of religion, 19, 117.

-association of Islam with violence, 45, 47.

-condemnation by religion, 111, 113.

-overcome religious violence, 19.

-rising in recent years, 112.

-sources of, 47, 112.

Weber, 61.

Westernization, 30, 103.

Women,

-discrimination agaist, 129, 140.

-equal rights and opportunities, 98.

-headscarf debate, 138.

-honor killing, 129, 141.

-inportance for democracy, 97.